Unbelievably Gross Jokes VOL. XXVII

Julius Alvin

Zebra Books
Kensington Publishing Corp.
http://www.zebrabooks.com

ZEBRA BOOKS are published by

Kensington Publishing Corp.
850 Third Avenue
New York, NY 10022

First Printing: August, 1998
10 9 8 7 6 5 4 3 2 1

Printed in the United States of America

GROSS-OUT GAGS—TOTALLY BEYOND BELIEF

Why hasn't a Polack won the Daytona 500?

Because they don't provide maps.

What do you call an armless man floating in the water?

Bob.

How do you save a man from drowning?

Take your foot off his head.

How do you make a blonde laugh on Saturday?

Tell her a joke on Wednesday.

Why do blondes hate M&M's?

They're too hard to peel.

How does a man show he's planning for the future?

He buys two cases of beer instead of one.

Why do men like love at first sight?

It saves them a lot of time.

Contents

One
Gross Animal and Vegetable Jokes

One day a guy started reading an article about bear hunting in an outdoor magazine. Although he'd never been anywhere outside the big city, he decided he wanted to become a bear hunter. He read everything he could about hunting bears, bought a gun, and headed into the wilderness. He set up a camp, hid in the woods at the edge of a stream, and waited.

Pretty soon, a huge grizzly walked into the stream to take a drink. The guy jumped out of the woods and fired. But he was too excited and missed badly. Just as he was about to fire again the bear looked at him and the guy froze in panic. Without a sound, the bear walked over to him, knocked the gun out of his hands, slapped him across the face, turned him around, pulled down his pants, and fucked him in the ass. When he was finished, the bear walked back into the woods.

Once he recovered, the guy was really pissed and vowed to get the bear, whatever it took. So, next hunting season, he set up in the same place and waited. Just like before, the giant grizzly lumbered into the stream. Again, the guy jumped out of the woods and took a shot. But, as before, he missed and froze in panic and the bear walked over to him, knocked the gun out of his hands, slapped him across the face, turned him around. and pulled down his pants. But this time he fucked him in the ass twice before he ambled off.

After he got out of the hospital, the guy was really steamed. He practiced shooting, took some courses in panic control, and headed back into the wilderness to blow the bear away. He hid in the woods by the stream, knowing the bear would return. And he did. But, like before, the guy jumped out of the woods and took a shot. Again, he missed and froze in panic. The bear shook his head in disgust and walked over to him, knocked the gun out of his hands, slapped him across the face, turned him around, and pulled down his pants.

Just before he was about to fuck him in the ass, the bear leaned over and whispered in his ear, "You don't really come here to hunt, do you?"

Why did the Polack break up with his girlfriend?

The damn sheep wanted a commitment.

What do you get when you cross a sheep and a talking parrot?

A great fuck, but it'll always want a cracker. And there's a chance it'll tell on you.

What's the best way to make a bull sweat?

Give him a tight Jersey.

Where do you get virgin wool?

From sheep that are too fast for the shepherd.

What's the best-selling sex toy in Ireland?

Inflatable sheep.

Did you hear about the queer Saint Bernards?

They got drunk and laid their paws on the table.

What's the difference between your fish and your meat?

If you beat your fish it's gonna die.

A guy is captured by band of Indians. They tie him to a stake and the chief gets ready to light the fire.

The guy yells, "HOLD IT, HOLD IT!!! Could I have one last request before you burn me."

The chief is surprised that this guy would even dare to make such a request, but thinks he has great courage, so he decides to listen.

"And what is your last request?"

"Could I talk to my horse?"

The chief agrees and they bring him his horse. The guy whispers in the horse's ear. The horse takes off over the hill, and in a couple minutes, comes back carrying a blonde on its back.

The chief smiles and says "Okay, I get it. I'll give you a half an hour with the girl."

The warriors untie the guy and he and the blonde go into the tent. A half hour later, they take the guy out and tie him up again. The chief starts to light the fire, but the guy again says, "Wait, can I have another request? Can I talk to my horse again, just one more time?"

The chief calls for the horse. The horse is brought again and again the guy whispers in its ear. The horse gallops over a hill and comes back with a brunette.

The chief nods his head and the warriors untie the guy and throw him in the teepee with the girl. A half an hour later, the guy is hauled out and tied to the stake. The chief raises his torch.

Again the guy yells, "One more request. This will be the last time.

The chief is pretty angry but says, "Okay, but this is it."

Naturally, he wants to see his horse. They bring it. The guy grabs it by its ears, shakes its head and whispers, "POSSE, you stupid asshole, POSSE. I want P-O-S-S-E, not PUSSY."

A farmer buys several pigs, hoping to breed them for ham and bacon. After several weeks, he notices that none of the pigs are getting pregnant, and calls a vet for help. The vet tells the farmer that he should try artificial insemination. The farmer doesn't have the slightest idea what this means but, not wanting to look like an ignorant cracker, he only asks the vet how he will know when the pigs are pregnant. The vet tells him that they will stop standing around and will, instead, lie down and wallow in the mud.

The farmer hangs up and gives it some thought. He comes to the conclusion that artificial insemination means he has to impregnate the pigs himself. So, he loads the pigs into his truck, drives them out into the woods, fucks them all, brings them back, and goes to bed. Next morning, he wakes and looks out at the pigs. Seeing that they are all still standing around, he concludes that the first try didn't take, and loads them in the truck again.

He drives them out to the woods, bangs each pig twice, for good measure, brings them back, and goes to bed. Next morning, he wakes to find the pigs still just standing around.

One more try, he tells himself, and proceeds to load them up and drive them out to the woods. He spends all day fucking the pigs and, upon returning home, falls listlessly into bed. The next morning, he's too tired to look out the window and see what's happening. He asks his wife to see if any are wallowing.

"No," she says, "but they're all in the truck, and one of them's honking the horn."

MARY HAD A LITTLE LAMB . . . UPDATED

Mary had a little lamb, its fleece was slightly gray,
It didn't have a father, just some borrowed DNA.
It sort of had a mother, though the ovum was on loan,
It was not so much a lambkin, as a little lamby clone.
And soon it had a fellow clone, and soon it had some more,
They followed her to school one day, all cramming through the door.
It made the children laugh and sing, the teachers found it droll,
There were too many lamby clones, for Mary to control.
No other could control the sheep, since their programs didn't vary,
So the scientists resolved it all, by simply cloning Mary.
But now they feel quite sheepish, those scientists unwary,
One problem solved, but what to do, with Mary, Mary, Mary . . .

What's gray and comes in quarts?

An elephant.

What did they call the guy after he drove a sled team all the way across Canada?

A husky fucker.

What's a sure way to teach a dog to fetch?

Tie a cat to a stick and throw it.

Where do you buy a secondhand dog?

At the used-cur dealer.

What's the most important thing to remember about fucking an elephant?

Never let her get on top.

Mary Riley, a devout Catholic spinster, decided to buy a parrot she'd seen at the pet store. But the owner was reluctant.

"Mary, that bird is not for you."

"Why," Mary asked, "she's beautiful."

"This bird has the dirtiest mouth in the entire country," said the owner.

"I'll straighten her out," said Mary, "You watch."

That night, she invited two priests from the local parish over for dinner. She uncovered her new bird to show it off. As soon as she removed the cover, the parrot piped up, "My name is Susie and I love to fuck like an animal."

Mary was mortified.

"Don't be upset, Mary" Father Flanagan said. "It's not your fault what this parrot has learned before you got her. We have two parrots, Peter and Paul, at our parsonage that we have trained to say the rosary. I'll be happy to take Susie to our place for a few days so she can live in the cage with these fine young birds and let them teach her their pious ways."

So Father Flanagan took Susie to the parsonage and put her in the cage with Peter and Paul. The two male parrots were fingering beads and reciting the rosary.

Suzie immediately squawked, "My name is Susie and I love to fuck like an animal!"

Peter said, "Awwkk! Drop the beads, Paul, our prayers have been answered!"

A commandant came to a French foreign legion post to inspect the troops and stay for a while. After an extensive tour of the grounds, the commandant noticed a tent at the far edge of the camp and asked, "What is housed there, captain?"

After stumbling on the words, the captain nervously replied, "Well, sir, you know how it is here—no women—life commitment to the post . . . well, ah, well, um, er, that is . . ."

"Well, what is it, captain?"

"Well, sir, the men have, well, they have . . . a . . . camel in there . . . and . . . they, well they you know they take the camel and they . . ."

"Stop right there, captain, I've heard enough—I don't want to hear any more about it. Such things going on in a legion's post!"

As time went by—one week, two weeks, a month, the commandant naturally began feeling the need for company. After he could take it no longer, the commandant approached the captain, asking, "Captain, do the troops still have that tent at camp's edge?

Shocked, the captain replied, "Yes, commandant."

"May I set up a time? How about this evening?"

"Yes, of course, commandant—I will arrange everything."

In the early morning hours, the commandant spotted the tent and entered. He saw a camel with a stool at its side. He positioned the stool, dropped his drawers, and began fucking the animal madly.

The captain, worried about the commandant after not seeing him for so long, made his way to the tent and entered thinking something was wrong.

When he saw what was happening, the captain said politely, "Wouldn't it be easier, commandant, to just ride it into town to meet the women, like the rest of us do?"

Why did the Polack cross the road?

His dick was still in the chicken.

Why did the chicken cross the road?

She was trying to get rid of the Polack.

What did the Polack's wife say when she saw the chicken on his dick?

You call that a rubber?

Two old ladies, Betty and Alice, were waiting for a bus. Betty was smoking a cigarette. It started to rain, so she reached into her purse, took out a condom, cut off the tip, slipped it over her cigarette, and continued to smoke.

Alice saw this and said, "Hey, that's a good idea! What is it that you put over your cigarette?"

Betty said, "It's a condom."

"A condom? Where do you get those?"

Betty told her friend that you could purchase condoms at the pharmacy. When the two old ladies arrived downtown, Alice went into the pharmacy and asked the pharmacist if he sold condoms. The pharmacist said yes, but looked a little surprised that this old woman was interested in condoms, so he asked her, "What size do you want?"

The old lady thought for a minute and said, "One that will fit a Camel."

This guy won a lot of money in the lottery and built the house of his dreams. It had everything, including a pool table. When everything was finished, he invited all his friends over to shoot a couple of games. One of his buddies brought a monkey. Before they could start to play, the monkey jumped onto the pool table and ate the cue ball. The guys thought about it for a second and realized the monkey would shit the cue ball eventually, and then they could clean it off and everything would be fine.

About a week later, the man with the monkey showed up with the cue ball. The monkey was very subdued and sat in a corner while they played a game. When they went up to the kitchen for lunch, the monkey jumped up on the counter and grabbed a bunch of grapes from a plate. He took one, looked at it, and shoved it up his ass. Then he took it out and ate it. He finished the entire bunch of grapes the same way—looking at one, sticking it up his ass, taking it out, and eating it.

"That's disgusting," said the homeowner, "What's going on with the monkey?"

"Simple," replied his friend, "Ever since he shit the cue ball, he measures everything he eats."

A cucumber and a pickle are having a conversation about how hard their lives are.

The pickle complains, "When I get big and fat and juicy they cover me with seasonings and stick me in a jar."

But the cucumber is unsympathetic, "Oh yeah? Big deal. When I get big and fat and juicy they slice me up and put me over a salad."

Just then a penis pokes his head up, "You think your life is so hard? When I get big and fat and juicy, they throw a plastic bag over my head, stick me in a dark, smelly room, and slide me up and down until I puke."

It was a warm, sunny Sunday, so a man and his wife decided to take in the zoo. They spent the day there, and at closing time, they walked past the gorilla cage, and the man noticed the gorilla looking at his wife.

"That gorilla is getting excited just looking at your tits," he said. "Why don't you take your blouse off and we'll see what he does?"

At first she declined. But, finally persuaded by her husband, she took off her blouse and bra. The gorilla went nuts. He started grunting and jumping up and down.

"Hey," the husband said, "Let's really blow his mind. Take off all your clothes and we'll see what he does."

Again, she said no and again he persuaded her. This time, the ape really went bananas! He climbed up and down the bars, did flips, ran around in circles, and tossed his food all over the cage. The husband went over to the cage, opened the door, and pushed his wife in.

"Now," said the husband with an evil smile, "Tell HIM you have a fucking headache!"

Three guys went out on Saturday night and got wasted big-time. When they went their separate ways, they were so blasted they couldn't see straight, but each remembered that they had agreed to get together the next afternoon.

The first guy said, "I was so drunk last night that on the way home, I laid down on the white line and let cars drive around me."

"That's nothing." said the second, "I broke into the gym and played basketball nude with the janitor."

"I got you both beat," said the third, "I got home OK, but I woke up this morning blowing chunks."

"What's the big deal about that," his friends said.

"Chunks is my dog," he replied.

A guy walked into his doctor's office scratching his crotch frantically.

"What's the problem?" asked the doctor.

"I got case of crabs because my brother's been fucking my wife behind my back," said the guy.

"Let's take a look," the doctor said.

"I'm gonna get rid of the mother fucker," the guy said, while the doctor was looking him over.

"You oughta get rid of the dog," said the doctor.

"Why?" said the puzzled man.

"Because you've got fleas," said the doctor.

The bartender was shutting a drunk off at the bar. The drunk was protesting.

"I can prove I'm not loaded," said the drunk.

"How?" said the bartender.

"See that cat coming in the door, he's only got one eye," said the drunk.

"That cat's going out the door buddy, and so are you," said the bartender.

Did you hear about the sheep who was a stripper?

She shears herself to raunchy music.

Why couldn't the stripper sheep make a living?

She could only work once a year.

What comes out of the cake at a Scottish bachelor party?

A sheep in sexy lingerie.

A Sunday golfer was preparing to hit to the tenth green. He took out his 8-iron got ready to swing. Just before he started, a voice said, "Take the 7." He looked around, saw nobody, and set himself to swing. Just as he was starting, the voice said again, "Use the 7."

This time he looked more carefully and saw a little green frog sitting on the ground saying, "Use the 7." The golfer put the 8-iron back in his bag, took the 7, swung, and the ball took off like a rocket, stopping four inches from the cup. For the rest of the afternoon, the frog hopped along with the golfer, telling him which clubs to use. The guy had the best round of his life, twenty strokes under his usual game.

As the golfer started to leave, the frog croaked, "Let's go to Atlantic City."

"Look, I'm grateful for your help. But, I've got a wife, children, a home. Dinner is all ready. Everyone is waiting for me. I can't go to Atlantic City."

The frog said, "Take me to Atlantic City. You won't be sorry."

So off they went to Atlantic City, and the player sat down at a blackjack table with the frog in his pocket. The first hand the player was dealt was a 17.

The frog said, "Hit it."

The player said, "Are you crazy. You stand on 17."

The frog said "Hit it." The player signaled the dealer to give him another card and got a 4.

By 3:00 A.M. the guy was ahead $480,000. And he was beat. He cashed in, and the hotel put him up in the suite reserved for extraordinarily large gamblers—free, of course. He also forgot to call his wife.

When the player and the frog got up to the room, the guy said, "I'm going to draw you a warm bath and you can sleep in a tub full of water."

The frog said, "I don't want to sleep in the tub. I want to sleep in the bed with you."

"Are you nuts? I'm not going to sleep with a frog."

"After what I've done for you, you owe me. . . . big-time."

The player decided, What the hell, it's only one night, and put the frog into bed with him.

He was just about to go to sleep when the frog said, "Kiss me."

"Wait a minute," the guy said, "I played the best round of golf in my life. I went to Atlantic City, made a ton of money. I got very lucky. Thank you very much, but I'm not kissing any frogs."

The frog said, "It wasn't luck. Kiss me!"

So the player said to himself, what the hell, and leaned over and kissed the frog. Lightning flashed and there was a lot of action in the bed. When the smoke cleared, in bed beside him was the most gorgeous, sexy, stark-naked, fourteen-year-old girl. The frog was no where in sight.

* * * * * *

"And I swear to you, Judge, that's just the way it happened, that's the truth, the whole truth, so help me God. That's exactly how I ended up in Atlantic City in bed with a fourteen-year-old girl."

Why do Scots love sheep so much?

After they fuck them, they can actually eat them.

What's rabbit fur in your teeth?

Pubic hare.

This guy was having a problem with mice in his apartment and was talking to his friend about it.

"I don't know what to do," he was saying. "I've tried everything and they won't go away. It's driving me nuts."

"I know what worked for me," the other guy said.

"Help me out," the first guy said, "I'll try anything."

"All you've gotta do is stuff steel wool in their little holes."

"That's it?" the first guy asked.

"That's it," said his friend.

About a week later, the guy calls his friend.

"How's it going with the mice?" he asks.

"Not so good," the guy says.

"What's the problem?" His friend asks.

"Well, first off, I'm having a lot of trouble holding their little legs apart."

Two

Really Gross Ethnic Jokes

A guy goes to his doctor and is told that he has six months to live.

"Six months!!" he exclaimed. "What can I do?"

"Marry a JAP and move to Montana," the doctor answered.

"Why?" the guy asked.

"Because six months will seem like an eternity!"

Why did the Polish hitman have to give up sex?

He took out his cock.

This black guy goes to the doctor for a vasectomy. Unlike the usual patients, he shows up in a limo, and he's sitting in the doctor's office in a rented tuxedo with black tie.

The doctor says "I've done a lot of these, but I've never seen a limo and tuxedo before. What's the story?"

The black guy looks at him and says, "If I'm gonna BE im-potent, I'm gonna LOOK im-potent!"

A small guy goes into an elevator, looks up, and notices a huge black dude standing next to him. The big black dude looks down upon the small guy and says, "7 feet tall, 350 pounds, 20-inch penis, 3-pound left testicle, 3-pound right testicle, Turner Brown."

The small guy faints.

The big dude picks up the small guy and brings him to, slapping his face and shaking him, and says, "What's wrong with you, honky?"

The small guy says, "Excuse me, but what did you say?"

The big black dude looks down and says, "7 feet tall, 350 pounds, 20-inch penis, 3-pound left testicle, 3-pound right testicle, Turner Brown."

The small guy says, "Thank God! I thought you said 'Turn around.' "

A man stumbled up to the only other patron in the bar and asked if he could buy him a drink. "Why, of course," was the reply.

The first man asked the second, "Where are you from?"

Said the second man, "I'm from Ireland."

The first man responded, "You don't say, *I'm* from Ireland, too! Let's have another round to Ireland."

Curious, the first man then asked, "Where in Ireland are you from?"

"Dublin," was the reply.

"I can't believe it," said the first man, "*I'm* from Dublin, let's have another drink to Dublin."

The second man replied, "Of course!"

Curiosity again struck, and the first man asked, "What school did you go to?"

The second man said, "Saint Mary's School."

"This is unbelievable," said the first man, "*I* went to

Saint Mary's School! I graduated in 1962. What year did you graduate?"

"Holy Mother of Mary, I graduated in 1962 as well!!!" exclaimed the second man.

The first man says," I just got out of jail."

"No kidding," the second man says. "So did I. What were you in for?"

"Fucking my brother," says the first.

"I can't believe it," says the second, "Me, too."

At about that time, one of the regulars came in and sat down at the bar.

"What's been going on?" he asked the bartender.

"Nothing much," replied the bartender, "the O'Malley twins are drunk again."

A marketing guy for a new firm had had a very bad week. Endless meetings in a half dozen cities, no sales. He was bummed, and just wanted to relax on his flight home from Kansas City. Luckily, it looked like he had all three seats to himself in his row, and he gratefully closed his eyes awaiting takeoff. At the last minute, another passenger plopped down beside him.

"Great, just great" he thought to himself. But then he opened his eyes and looked to see an absolutely gorgeous woman, blonde, green eyes, maybe 5 feet 4 inches tall, nicely built, well-groomed, and well-dressed.

Hmm, he thought, maybe my luck is going to change. She also still had a name tag on from something. So he turned to her and said "Hi, Masra. Are you traveling alone?"

She laughed and said "Oh, that's not my name. I was the keynote speaker at a convention today and forgot to take the silly thing off. It stands for Midwest American Sexual Response Association."

"Keynote huh? That sounds fascinating. What was your speech about?"

"Well, I'm a licensed sex therapist, and have been doing research on the ability of the American male to please women. I've discovered that the American male, contrary to many people's uninformed opinions, is actually quite a good lover. However, there are three groups of Americans that really stand out from the crowd.

"One group is Jewish men, because they seem to be able to really talk with women. Then, Native Americans, because they're so well built. The third are men from the South, because of the size of their cocks."

And by the way, my name's Wanda. What's yours?"

"Hi, Wanda. I'm Tonto Rosenberg, but all my friends down home just call me Bubba."

What do you say to a black man in a three-piece suit?

Will the defendant please rise.

Why did the Puerto Rican pee in his coffee every morning?

He heard there was sugar in urine.

This investment banker came back early from work one day and found his wife lying buck-nude and spread-eagled in the bed. He noticed a cigar butt in the ashtray.

"Where'd that cigar come from." he asked. A Polack yuppie jumped out of the closet and proudly said, "Cuba."

How can you tell if blacks are living in the house next door?

The cockroaches eat out.

What do you call a black man in a BMW?

A car thief.

Why did they move the Polack cop out of the traffic division?

He kept giving speeding tickets to parked cars.

Why do Puerto Rican dogs have stubby noses?

From chasing parked cars.

Why did the Polish drug addict never get high?

He kept shooting junk mail.

Why did the Polish woman have to stop using her dildo?

Telephone poles have slivers.

Why did the Puerto Rican hold his letters to his ear?

Somebody told him he had voice mail.

The barber finished giving a priest a hair cut. The priest pulled out his wallet and reached for some bills.

"Oh, no, Father," the barber said, "I never charge a man of the cloth."

The priest was very moved by his generosity, and the next morning the barber found a case of nice Italian wine on his doorstep.

The next day a baptist minister walked in for a hair cut and the same thing happened. When he offered to pay, the barber refused, saying, "Oh no, Reverend, I never charge a man of the cloth."

The minister was moved by his generosity, and the next morning had his wife send over a big container of her finest barbecued ribs.

Then a Rabbi came in for a hair cut and the same thing happened again. When he offered to pay, the barber said, "Oh, no, Rabbi, I never charge a man of the cloth."

The next morning when the barber opened his door there were twelve Rabbis standing there.

Did you hear about the gay guy who was half-French and half-Greek?

He didn't know which way to turn.

Why did the Polack stop using his toilet brush?

Paper didn't scratch his ass as much.

Why did the Polack want to hang out in the bathroom of the Irish bar?

He heard people were tossing cookies in there all the time.

What's a toilet full of barf to a Polack?

Cold soup.

Why are there always flies buzzing around Sadam Hussein's head?

Because he's got shit for brains.

Why did the Puerto Rican hold his cat in the shower?

Because he heard a good pussy was soft and warm and wet.

Why couldn't the Irishman composer finish his song?

He kept passing out after the first eight bars.

How did the black guy entertain himself in prison?

He did the Macarena to his arrest record.

What's another name for a hillbilly shepherd?

The local pimp.

Why did the plastic surgeon give up on the Polack?

She kept picking her own nose.

Why did the Puerto Rican janitor like living in the bathroom?

He didn't have to pay rent, and had all the shit he could eat.

How can you tell a group of Polish duck hunters?

They're the ones blasting away at their decoys.

Why is a Polack uncomfortable in a fancy restaurant?

There's all this silverware but no can opener.

How does an Irishman tell if the vegetables are fresh?

If the label isn't peeled on the can.

Why didn't the Polack make it as a hijacker?

He was afraid to fly.

Why did the Polish record producer get his house blown up?

He signed a band of terrorists.

Why did the Polish terrorist fill the envelope with Tidy Cat?
He was making a litter bomb.

Why did the Polish kidnapper clean out his savings account?

It was the only way to get his daughter back alive.

Why did Mohammed get fired as a taxi driver?

He learned English.

Who invented the telephone pole?

Alexander Graham Bellinski

Why did the Polack keep driving into walls during driver's ed?

They'd told him it was a crash course.

So there's this fella with a parrot. And this parrot swears like a sailor, I mean he's a pistol. He can swear for five minutes straight without repeating himself. Trouble is, the guy who owns him is a quiet, conservative type, and this bird's foul mouth is driving him crazy.

One day, it gets to be too much, so the guy grabs the bird by the throat, shakes him really hard, and yells, "QUIT IT!" But this just makes the bird mad, and he swears more than ever.

Then the guy gets mad and says, "OK, for you," and locks the bird in a kitchen cabinet. This really aggravates the bird, and he claws and scratches, and when the guy finally lets him out, the bird cuts loose with a stream of invectives that would make a veteran sailor blush.

At that point, the guy is so mad that he throws the bird into the freezer.

For the first few seconds, there's a terrible racket. The bird kicks and claws and thrashes. Then it suddenly gets very quiet.

The guy starts to think that the bird may be hurt. After a couple of minutes of silence, he's so worried that he opens up the freezer door.

The bird calmly climbs onto the man's out-stretched arm and says, "Awfully sorry about the trouble I gave you. I'll do my best to improve my vocabulary from now on."

The man is astounded. He can't believe what's come over the parrot.

Then the parrot says, "By the way, you cocksucker, how do chickens deal with the fucking freezer?"

Three
Totally Offensive Lawyer and Doctor Jokes

"Doctor," the nervous woman cried, "can you get pregnant from anal intercourse?"

"Certainly," replied the doctor, "Where do you think lawyers come from?"

For several years, a lawyer had been going to a secluded inn for his vocation because the innkeeper's daughter was really hot, and he was dying to get in her pants. Finally, he managed to fuck her, and it was everything he dreamed of. He couldn't wait to get back the next year for another round of pussy.

The next year, he arrived at the inn in a state of frenzied excitement. The innkeeper welcomed him warmly and said there was something special waiting in his room. When he opened the door he saw the object of his lust sitting in a rocking chair holding a baby and smiling at him.

Lust instantly became love, and he cried, "Darling, why didn't you tell me. We'll get married and the baby will have my name."

"Oh, don't be silly," the beautiful young woman sighed. "My father and I decided it would be better to have a bastard in the family than a fucking lawyer."

A grade school teacher was asking students what their parents did for a living. "Johnny, you be first," she said. "What does your mother do all day?"

Johnny stood up and said, "She's a doctor."

"That's wonderful. How about you, Jane?"

Jane said, "My father is a mailman."

"Thank you, Jane," said the teacher, "That's wonderful, too."

"What about your father, Billy?"

Billy proudly stood up and announced, "My daddy plays piano in a faggot whorehouse."

The teacher was shocked, and went to Billy's house after school. Billy's father answered the door. The teacher explained what his son had said and demanded an explanation.

Billy's father shrugged and said, "I'm really a lawyer, but how do you admit something like that to a child?"

Q: What's the difference between a lawyer and a bucket of shit?

A: The bucket.

Q: What can a goose do, a duck can't, and a lawyer should?

A: Stick his bill up his ass.

Q. What's the difference between a lawyer and a gigolo?

A. A gigolo only fucks one person at a time.

Q. Why do lawyers wear neckties?

A. To keep the foreskin from crawling up their chins.

Q: If you saw your lawyer fucking someone in the back of your car, what's the first thing you should do?

A: See if it's your wife.

This guy's wife is having a lot of pain during her pregnancy. They go to the doctor, and the man says, "I only wish I could carry the pain for a while, but I know I can't."

The doctor says, "No, wait. I have a machine that transfers the pain that the mother feels to the father."

The man says, "That's great! I'll try it."

So they hook him up and the doctor turns on the machine. The man says, "I don't feel anything."

The doctor says, "Hmmm, I better turn it up some more."

Still the man doesn't feel anything. So the doctor turns it up more. And still nothing. So the doctor turns it up to the highest level and says "Normally this would kill a man."

The man says, "Strange, I still don't feel anything."

The husband and wife go home from the doctor's office and find the mailman dead on their doorstep.

Patient: I'm in a hospital! Why am I in here?

Doctor: You were in a terrible accident.

Patient: What happened?

Doctor: Well, I've got some good news and some bad news. Which would you like to hear first?

Patient: Well . . . The bad news first. . . .

Doctor: Your legs were injured so badly that we had to amputate both of them.

Patient: That's terrible! What's the good news?

Doctor: The guy in the next bed wants to buy your slippers.

Doctor: I have some good news and I have some bad news, which shall I tell first?

Patient: The bad news I guess.

Doctor: All right. Your son has drowned, your daughter has been raped, your wife has divorced you. Your house got blown away, and you have AIDS.

Patient: Good grief! What's the good news?

Doctor: The good news is that there is no more bad news.

A young man, on his first visit to a big city, decides to go visit the local whorehouse. A little while later, he starts to feel sick. He goes to see a doctor of internal medicine.

The doctor examines him and says, "Well, son, I don't know how to tell you this, but you've got a bad case of syphilis, gonorrhea, and about twelve other things I can't spell. I'm afraid I'm going to have to give you this medicine. It'll make you get better, but it'll also cause your penis to shrivel up and disappear. It's going to cost you $1000."

The man wants a second opinion so he goes and sees a surgeon.

The surgeon examines him and says "Sorry, but it looks like syphilis, gonorrhea, and a few other things to boot. Afraid I'm going to have to cut your dick off and charge you $2,000."

By this time, the guy is desperate so he goes to see a doctor of holistic medicine. The holistic doctor comes to the same conclusion, it's a serious case of VD but he tells the man his cure will only cost $50.

"That's great. What shall I do," the man asks.

"Go home and eat lots of good food, get plenty of rest, and gets lots of sunshine and fresh air. Wait about two weeks and your dick will fall off all by itself."

A woman went to a doctor with a problem, but she was too embarrassed to talk about it. Eventually, the doctor managed to discover that she thought she was sexually perverted.

"What sort of perversion are you talking about?" asked the doctor.

"Well," said the woman, "I like to be . . . Ohh . . . Ah . . . Ummm . . . I'm sorry doctor, but I'm too ashamed to talk about it."

"Come, come, my dear, I'm a doctor. What's the matter? . . ."

But she couldn't do it. So the doctor said, "Look, I'm a little kinky myself. I'll show you mine if you show me yours."

The woman considered the offer, and agreed that it might make it easier. So she said "Well, I like to be kissed all over my ass."

"Is that all?" said the doctor. "Go behind that screen, take all your clothes off."

So the woman undressed behind the screen and waited. Fifteen minutes pass and nothing had happened. So the woman peeked around the side of the screen and saw the doctor sitting behind his desk, his feet up on the table, reading a newspaper and whistling to himself.

"Hey!" shouted the woman, "I thought you said you were a pervert?"

"Oh I am," said the doctor, "I just took a shit in your handbag."

Three Jewish mothers are bragging about their sons.

The first one says "My son is very successful. He is the best lawyer in New York City."

The second one says "My son has done better than that. He is the best doctor in New York City."

The third one says "My son hasn't done that well. He doesn't have a job, and he's gay."

"That's terrible," the others sighed smugly.

"But," she continued, "He has these two great boyfriends. One is the best lawyer in New York City, and the other is the best doctor."

"How did it happen?" the doctor asked the middle-aged farmhand as he set the man's broken leg.

"Well, doc, 25 years ago . . ."

"Never mind the past. Tell me how you broke your leg this morning."

"Like I was saying . . . It was right after I got hired some twenty-five years ago. I'd done my work and gone to bed. The farmer's daughter came into my room. She asked me if there was anything I wanted. I said no, everything is fine. "Are you sure?" she asked. "I'm sure, I said. "Isn't there anything I can do for you?" she wanted to know. "I reckon not," I replied. . . .

"Excuse me," said the doctor, "What does this story have to do with your leg?"

"Well, this morning," the farmhand explained, "when I figured out what she was talking about, I fell right off the roof of the barn."

A doctor on his rounds in a mental hospital sees a couple of patients behaving strangely. The first man is sitting on the edge of his bed, clutching an imaginary steering wheel and making loud noises: VRROOOOM, VRRROOOOMM . . . SCREEEECH . . .

"What are you doing?" asks the doctor.

"I'm taking this big ole' eighteen wheeler down to Memphis," replies the patient.

The man in the next bed is under the covers, and the bed is shaking wildly. The doctor pulls the covers back and sees that the guy is totally naked and jerking off into the mattress.

"What are you doing?" asks the doctor, a little perplexed.

"Well," pants the man, "While he's on his way to Memphis, I'm fucking his wife."

A man goes to the doctor and says, "Doc, I'd like to live a long time. What should I do?"

"Good plan," the doctor replies. "Do you smoke?"

"Oh . . . Half a pack a day."

"Starting now, no more smoking."

The man agrees.

The doctor then asks, "Do you drink?"

"Oh, well Doc, not much, just a bit of wine with my meals, and a beer or two every once in a while."

"Starting now, you drink only water. No exceptions."

The man is a bit upset, but also agrees.

The doctor asks, "What kind of things do you eat?"

"Oh, well, you know, Doc, normal stuff."

"Starting now you're on a very strict diet: raw vegetables with no dressing, and nonfat cottage cheese."

"Doc, is all this really necessary?"

"Do you want to live a long time?"

"Yes."

"Absolutely necessary. And don't even think of breaking the diet."

The doctor continues, "Do you have sex?"

"Yeah, once a week or so . . . , only with my wife!" he adds hurriedly.

"As soon as you get out of here you are going to separate bedrooms. No more sex for you. None."

The man is appalled. "Doc . . . Are you sure I'm going to live longer this way?"

"You got me, but I can tell you that, however long it is, it's going to seem like a fucking eternity."

A man and a woman were talking in a hospital waiting room.

Man: "What are you doing here today?"

Woman: "Oh, I'm here to donate some blood. They're going to give me five dollars for it."

Man: "Hmm, that's interesting. I'm here to donate sperm, myself. But they pay me twenty-five dollars."

The woman looked thoughtful for a moment and they chatted some more before going their separate ways. Several months later, the same man and woman met again in the same waiting room.

Man: "Oh, hi there! Here to donate blood again?"

Woman: [shaking her head with her mouth closed] "Unh unh."

While doing a vasectomy, the doctor slipped and cut off one of a man's balls. Thinking quickly, he replaced the missing ball with an onion. Several weeks later, the patient returned for a checkup.

"How's your sex life?" the doctor asked.

"Pretty good," the man said, to the doctor's relief. But then he added, "I've had some strange side effects."

"What's that?" the doctor asked anxiously.

"Well, every time I piss, my eyes water. When my wife gives me a blow job, she gets heartburn. And every time I pass a hamburger stand, I get a hard-on."

A woman goes to her doctor, who verifies that she is pregnant. This is her first pregnancy. The doctor asks her if she has any questions.

She replies, "Well, I'm a little worried about the pain. How much will childbirth hurt?"

The doctor answered, "Well, that varies from woman to woman, and pregnancy to pregnancy, and beside, it's difficult to describe pain."

"I know, but can't you give me some idea?," she asks.

"Grab your upper lip and pull it out a little. . . ."

"Like this?"

"A little more. . . ."

"Like this?"

"No. A little more. . . ."

"Like this?"

"Yes. Does that hurt?"

"Damn right."

"Now stretch it over your head!"

A woman goes to the dentist. As he leans over to begin working on her, she grabs his balls.

The dentist says, "Why did you grab my nuts."

The woman replies, "Just to make sure we don't hurt each other."

A woman is lying on a gurney out in a hospital hall prior to going to surgery. As she lies there, a man in a white coat comes by, lifts up the sheet, and then leaves. This happens a second time. The third time this happens, she says "Doctor, am I going into surgery soon?"

The man replied, "Don't ask me lady. I'm just a painter!"

There was a country doctor who was the only doctor for miles around. He wanted to go on a fishing trip, so he called the vet and asked him to look after things while he was gone. The vet asked, "Is anything happening?"

The doctor replied, "Mrs. Jones is about due, but I don't think the baby will come before I get back. Anyway, if it does, just deliver it. This is her third, and the first two went really easily."

The vet said "OK" and the doctor went on the fishing trip. When he returned, he called the vet.

"How did things go while I was gone?"

"Pretty good."

"Did Mrs. Jones have her baby?"

"Yes, it was an eight pound boy. Everyone's doing fine."

"Did you have any trouble?"

"Well, there was just one little problem."

"What was that?"

"I had a rough time getting her to eat the afterbirth!"

Everywhere Bertha went, nobody wanted to talk to her, no one ever asked her to go out. Guys came up to her, and turned away. So she went to her doctor and told him what was going on. The doctor told her he would give her a complete exam. He told her to undress and get up on the table. He told her to open her mouth, and he checked it. Then he asked her to get down from the table and bend over.

Later, in his office, the doctor said, "Know what your problem is, Bertha?"

"What ?"

"Your mouth smells exactly like your asshole."

After much soul-searching, a childless couple decided to try artificial insemination. When the woman showed up at the clinic, she was told to undress from the waist down, get on the table, and place her feet in the stirrups. She was feeling uncomfortable enough already, when she saw the doctor coming in unzipping his pants.

"Wait a minute! What the hell is going on here?" cried the woman, pulling herself into a sitting position.

"Don't you want to get pregnant?" asked the doctor.

"Well, yes, I do," answered the woman.

"Then lie back and spread 'em," replied the doctor. "We're all out of the bottled stuff. You'll just have to settle for what's on tap."

This German guy wants to marry this Polish lady, but Poland has a law that you have to be Polish in order to marry someone Polish. At the embassy, they told him he'd have to have 50% of his brain removed. So he goes to his doctor and says, "I've just GOT to marry this woman, I love her so much. . . ."

So the doctor says, "Well, it's risky, but okay."

When the guy comes out of surgery, the doctor walks in and says, "We're sorry, but we accidentally removed 75% of your brain instead of 50%."

The guy looks up and says, "Mama mia!"

This guy goes into a doctor's office and says "Doctor, doctor, you've gotta help me. I just can't stop having sex!"

"Well how often do you have it?" the doctor asks.

"Well, twice a day I have sex with my wife."

"That's not so much," says the doctor.

"Yes, but that's not all. Twice a day I have sex with my secretary," replies the man.

"Well that is probably a bit excessive," says the doctor.

"Yes, but that's not all. Twice a day I have sex with a prostitute," says the man.

"Well, that's definitely too much," says the doctor. "You've got to learn to take yourself in hand."

"I do," cried the man. "Twice a day."

A group of psychiatrists tour an insane asylum that is renowned for their progressive rehabilitation methods. They begin by visiting some of the patients. The first patient they visit is a young woman. She is practicing ballet.

One of the psychiatrist asks, "What are you doing?" She replies, "I'm studying ballet so when I get out of here, I can possibly join a troupe and be a productive member of society."

"Wow, that's wonderful."

The next person was a man reading a book with a pile of books next to him. The same question was asked, "What are you doing?"

"I'm studying biology and chemistry so I can enter medical school when I get out."

Finally, they reached a room in the asylum but the director wouldn't open the door. The group insisted, and finally, he did. Inside was a man balancing a peanut on his cock.

"My God, what are you doing?" the group asked.

The man replied: "I'm fucking nuts, and I'm never getting out of here."

Two guys are walking through the woods. Suddenly, a snake bites one of the guys on his cock. His friend has a cel phone and calls his doctor.

"My friend has just been bitten by a snake," he tells the doctor, "What should I do?"

The doctor asks him to describe the snake. After he does, the doctor tells him there's no time to waste and that he has to suck the poison out immediately. The guy hangs up his cel phone and turns to his friend.

"What did he say?" whispers his friend weakly.

"You'll be dead in half an hour."

Q: How many doctors does it take to screw in a light-bulb?

A: That depends on whether it has health insurance.

A: Three. One to find a bulb specialist, one to find a bulb installation specialist, and one to bill it all to Medicare.

A: None. They would wait for a suitable donor and do a filament transplant.

How is an undertaker like a bottle of Robitussin?

They both take away the coffin.

A girl goes into the doctor's office for a checkup. As she takes off her blouse, he notices a red "H" on her chest.

"How did you get that mark on your chest?" asks the doctor.

"Oh, my boyfriend went to Harvard, and he's so proud of it that he never takes off his Harvard sweatshirt, even when we make love," she replies.

A couple of days later, another girl comes in for a checkup. As she takes off her blouse, he notices a blue "Y" on her chest.

"How did you get that mark on your chest?" asks the doctor.

"Oh, my boyfriend went to Yale and he's so proud of it that he never takes off his Yale sweatshirt, even when we make love," she replies.

A couple of days later, another girl comes in for a checkup. As she takes off her blouse, he notices a green "M" on her chest.

"Do you have a boyfriend at Michigan?" asks the doctor.

"No, but I have a girlfriend at Wisconsin. Why do you ask?"

This guy had been suffering from excruciating headaches for some time, and finally went to a doctor. After a thorough exam, the doctor said, "Well, I'm not exactly sure what is causing your headaches, but we've found a cure for them—you'll have to be castrated."

Naturally, the man told his doctor that he would try to bear the pain. But as time went on, the headaches only got worse, and finally, the poor fellow was driven back to the doctor. "All right, I guess I'll have the operation," he said.

When it was all over, the man was understandably depressed, and his physician told him, "I recommend you start a new life, you'll just have to learn how to go on from here."

So the man decided to take the advice, and went to a men's shop for a new set of clothes.

The tailor said, "Starting with the suit, looks like you take about a 38-regular."

"That's right," exclaimed the man, "How'd you know?"

"Well, when you've been in the business as long as I have, you get pretty good at sizing a man up," replied the salesman. "Now, for a shirt, looks like about a 15-inch neck and a 33-inch sleeve."

"Right again," the man said.

"And for underwear, I'd say a size 36."

"There's your first mistake," the man said, "I've worn 32s for years."

"No, you're a size 36, if I've ever seen one," said the owner.

The man replied, "I ought to know what size underwear I wear, and I'll take 32s."

"Well all right, if you insist, but they're going to pinch your balls and give you headaches!!"

A woman went to her doctor for a follow-up visit after the doctor had prescribed testosterone for her. She was a little worried about some of the side effects she was experiencing.

"Doctor, the hormones you've been giving me have really helped, but I'm afraid that you're giving me too much. I've started growing hair in places where I've never grown hair before."

The doctor reassured her. "A little hair growth is a perfectly normal side effect of testosterone. Just where has this hair appeared?"

"On my balls," she answered.

After her husband told her that her pussy was too big, a woman went to see her doctor. The doctor put her up on the table and took a look. After a moment of stunned silence the doctor shouted, "What a giant pussy!! What a giant pussy!!"

"Did you have to say it twice," the angry woman shrieked.

"Lady," the doctor replied, "I didn't, it was the echo."

This young couple had only been married for about two weeks when the wife complained of a burning sensation in her chest. She told her husband, who suggested that she go to the doctor. She made an appointment and went the following day.

The doctor called the husband at work saying, "I have to tell your wife that she has acute angina. . . ."

"Yeah, I know, she's got a great set of tits, too!"

Four

Disgusting Married Jokes

The couple had been married for thirty years, and on their anniversary they decided to go back to the same hotel where they had spent their blissful wedding night.

Her husband was lying on the bed when she came out of the bathroom totally nude, just as she had thirty years before. She stood seductively before him and asked, "Tell me, darling, what were you thinking thirty years ago when I came out of the bathroom like this?"

He replied, "I took one look at you and thought I'd like to screw your brains out and suck your boobs dry."

"And what are you thinking now, baby?" she asked huskily.

He said, "I'm thinking I did a damn good job."

A man was taking his wife, who was pregnant with twins, to the hospital when his car went out of control and crashed. Upon regaining consciousness, he saw his brother, a relentless world-class practical joker, sitting at his bedside.

He asked his brother how his wife was and his brother replied, "Don't worry, everybody is fine, and you have a son and a daughter. But the hospital was in a real hurry to get the birth certificates filed, and both you and your wife were unconscious, so I named them for you."

The husband asked, "OK, what did you name them?"

The brother replied, "I named the little girl Denise."

The husband said, "That's a very pretty name! What did you come up with for my son?"

The brother replied, "Denephew."

A married couple retire to their hotel room on their wedding night. The man, who is much larger than the petite woman, takes off his pants and throws them over to his wife, saying, "Put these on."

The woman replies "But they are too big for me. . . ."

"Put them on, anyway"

She puts them on, they fall down, and she says "I can't fit into these. . . ."

He replies "That's right, now just remember who wears the pants in this family."

The woman then takes off her panties and throws them over to her husband, saying, "Put these on."

He looks at them and says "I can't get into these. . . ."

She replies "Yes, that's right. And you won't be able to in the future unless you change your fucking attitude!"

After a few years of married life, this guy finds that he can't get it up anymore. He goes to his doctor, and his doctor tries a few things, but nothing works.

Finally the doctor says to him, "This is all in your mind," and refers him to a psychiatrist. After he visits the shrink, the shrink confesses, "I am at a loss as to how you could possibly be cured."

Finally the psychiatrist refers him to witch doctor.

The witch doctor tells him, "I can cure this," and throws some powder on a flame, and there is a flash with billowing blue smoke. . . . The witch doctor says, "This is powerful healing but you can only use it once a year. All you have to do is say 'one, two, three,' and it shall rise for as long as you wish."

The guy then asks the witch doctor "What happens when it's over?" The witch doctor says "All you have to say is 'one, two, three, four,' and it will go down. But be warned, it will not work again for a year!"

When the guy goes home and that night, he is ready to surprise his wife with the good news. . . . So, he is lying in bed with her and says "one, two, three," and suddenly he gets an erection.

His wife turns over and says "What did you say 'one, two, three,' for?"

A woman was in bed with her lover when she heard her husband opening the front door. "Hurry!" she said, "Stand in the corner." She quickly rubbed baby oil all over him and then she dusted him with talcum powder. "Don't move until I tell you to," she whispered. "Just pretend you're a statue."

"What's this, honey?" the husband inquired as he entered the room.

"Oh, it's just a statue," she replied nonchalantly. "The Smiths bought one for their bedroom. I liked it so much, I got one for us, too." No more was said about the statue, not even later that night when they went to sleep.

Around two in the morning the husband got out of bed, went to the kitchen, and returned a while later with a sandwich and a glass of milk.

"Here," he said to the 'statue,' "Eat something. I stood like an idiot at the Smithses' for three days, and nobody offered me as much as a glass of water."

A guy on a date parks his car and gets the girl in the back seat. They make love, but the girl wants it again, and the guy complies. She wants more, and they do it again. She still wants more, and the guy says "Excuse me a minute, I have to relieve myself." While out of the car he notices a man half a block away changing a flat.

He says to the man "Look, I've got this chick in my car, and I've given it to her four or five times, and she still wants more. I'll change your flat if you'll take over for me."

So that's what the man does, and he about to cum

when a cop knocks on the window and shines a light on them.

The cop asks, "What are you doing in there?"

The guy says, "I'm making love to my wife."

The cop asks, "Why don't you do that at home?"

The guy answers, "To tell you the truth, I didn't know it was my wife until you shined the light on her."

Jeb's hillbilly wife decided she wanted to do something special to please him when he came home from his long hunting trip with Zeb, so she bought a pair of crotchless panties. That night, as he came into the house, she lay sprawled on the couch spread-eagled.

"Hi, honey," she purred sexily. "Y'all want some of this?"

"Hell no!" he roared. "Look at what it done done to your undies."

The couple visited a sex clinic to complain that their sex life had become a bore. Each night, the man would arrive home. His wife would prepare supper. After supper, they'd watch two hours of television. Immediately afterward, they would go to bed. From that point on, every move was routine.

"No wonder," the sex therapist said. "You've made sex monotonous. Stop living on a schedule. Get into sex whenever you feel like it. Don't wait until bedtime each night to do it. Do it whenever you get into the mood."

The couple agreed to try the advice. They returned the following week. "How did things work out?" the sex therapist asked.

The man and his wife were beaming. "It worked! It worked great!!!"

"Tell me about it," said the therapist.

"Well, two nights after we saw you, we were eating supper when I noticed I had this huge boner. So I didn't wait for any shower or any television. I reached out, ripped off her blouse and bra. Then I tore off her panties. I flung her right onto the table, spilling all the wine and soup. Then I unzipped, and we had sex like we've never had it before!!"

"That's wonderful!!" said the sex therapist. "I told you it would work if you did it when the spirit moved you!"

"Only one thing," said the man a little sadly. "They're not ever going to let us go back into that restaurant."

A man and his wife were stranded on a deserted island for many years. One day a new guy washed up on shore. He immediately started hitting on the man's wife and the wife was into it, but they knew they'd have to be careful.

The husband was excited to have someone new around. "This is great he said, "Now we've got three people to split the shifts in the watchtower." The new guy agreed to take the first shift. He climbed up to the tower and started looking around while the husband and wife started placing stones in a circle for a cooking fire.

"Hey, no fucking down there," he yelled.

"We're not fucking," they yelled back, and started putting driftwood into the stone circle.

Again, the new guy yelled down, "Hey, I said no fucking."

Again, they yelled back, "We're not fucking."

After lunch, they started to repair the roof on their hut.

Once again, the new guy yelled down, "Hey, I said no fucking."

"We told you, we're not fucking. Look for ships," the shouted back.

"It sure looks like it from here," the new guy yelled back.

Finally his shift was over and the new guy climbed down from the tower. The husband crawled up to replace him. The minute he was gone, the new guy and the wife were fucking like monkeys.

The husband looked down and shouted, "Hey, are you fucking.?"

"No," they called back, "We're fixing the fence."

"Son of a bitch," said the husband to himself. "From up here it really does look like people are fucking."

A newlywed couple were on their honeymoon. Before hopping into bed, the bride said to the groom, "Honey, please be careful. . . . I'm a virgin."

"What in the hell do you mean by that?" the guy said, "I'm your third husband."

His bride smiled sweetly and replied, "Well, my first husband was a psychologist and all he wanted to do was talk about it, my second husband was a gynecologist and all he wanted to do was look at it, and since you are a lawyer, I know I'll get screwed!"

A husband and wife were lying in bed. The husband reached over and nudged his wife.

She said "What do you want?"

He said "You know."

She said, "Can't, I have to see my gynecologist tomorrow."

He said, "Oh."

Later, the husband reached over and nudged his wife again.

She said, "I told you I had to see my doctor tomorrow."

He said, "But you don't have to see your dentist, do you?"

DO YOU KNOW JACK SHIT?

Jack Shit is the only son of Awe Shit, the fertilizer magnet who married Oh Shit, the owner of Kneedeepin Shit Inn. Jack Shit married No Shit, and they produced six children. Holy Shit, their first, passed on shortly after birth. Next came twin sons, Deep Shit and Dip Shit; two daughters, Fulla Shit and Giva Shit; and another son, Bull Shit. Deep Shit married Dumb Shit, a high school dropout. Dip Shit married Lotta Shit and they have a son, Chicken Shit. Fulla Shit and Giva Shit married the Happens brothers. The Shit-Happens children are Dawg Shit, Byrd Shit, and Cow Shit. Bull Shit just married his second cousin, Piecea Shit. They now await the arrival of a child they're going to call Little Shit.

Now you can say you know "Jack Shit."

A HUSBAND'S LETTER TO HIS WIFE

Dear Betty,

During the past year, I have attempted to make love to you 365 times. I have succeeded 36 times, which is an average of only once every 10 days. The following is a list of why I didn't succeed more often:

Wake the kids	14 times
Too late	15 times
Too tired	42 times
Too early	13 times
Too hot	19 times
Pretending to be asleep	49 times
The neighbors will hear	20 times
Headache and backache	29 times

Sunburn	11 times
Mother will hear us	10 times
Not in the mood	22 times
Watching Leno	18 times
Too sore	26 times
New Hairdo	6 times
Wrong time of the month	15 times
Had to go to the bathroom	20 times

The 36 times we did make it were not necessarily great; for instance: 6 times you just laid there, 8 times you reminded me that there was a crack in the ceiling, 4 times you told me to hurry and get it over with, 7 times I had to wake you to tell you I had finished, and once I was afraid I had hurt you, because you started thrashing around and breathing heavily.

Love, John

A WIFE'S LETTER TO HER HUSBAND

Dear John,

I think things are a little confused. Here are the real reasons you didn't get more than you did:

Came home drunk and screwed the cat	15 times
Did not come home at all	36 times
Did not come	22 times
Came too soon	34 times
Lost your boner	20 times
Cramps in your legs	17 times
Worked too late	37 times
Had a rash	30 times
Caught your dick in your zipper	16 times
Had a cold	22 times
Burned your tongue	10 times
Splinter in your finger	2 times
Lost the urge	42 times

Came in your shorts after reading a dirty book 16 times

The reason I lay still was because you missed me and were fucking the sheets. You seemed to be having such a good time, I didn't want to move and ruin it for you. I wasn't talking about the crack in the ceiling—what I said was "Would you like me on my back or kneeling?" The time I was thrashing around was because you farted and I was fighting for air.

Love, Betty

Five
Ugly Kid, Cripple, and Blonde Jokes

One day, the teacher walks into her classroom and announces to the class that on each Friday, she will ask a question to the class, and anyone who answers correctly doesn't have to go to school the following Monday.

On the first Friday, the teacher asks, "How many grains of sand are on the beach?" Needless to say, no one could answer.

The following Friday, the teacher asks the class, "How many stars are in the sky?" and again no one could answer. Frustrated, little Johnny decides that the next Friday he would somehow answer the question and get a three-day weekend.

So, Thursday night, Johnny takes two ping-pong balls and paints them black. The next day, he brings them to school in a paper bag. At the end of the day, just when the teacher says, "Here's this week's question," Johnny empties the bag to the floor, sending the ping-pong balls rolling to the front of the room. Because they are young kids who find any disruption of class amusing, the entire class starts laughing.

The teacher says, "Okay, who's the comedian with the black balls?"

Immediately, little Johnny stands up and says, "Bill Cosby, see ya on Tuesday!"

DEAD BABIES AND PITCHFORKS

Q: What's easier to unload, a truck full of dead babies or a truckful of bowling balls?

A: Dead Babies because you can use your pitchfork.

Q: What's the difference between a truckful of water and a truckful of babies?

A: You can't move water with a pitchfork.

Q: Why do you want to unload a truckful of dead babies with a pitchfork?

A: So you can tell if any are still alive.

Q: How do you know when you've hit a live one?

A: The pitchfork shakes.

Q: How do you find a live baby in a pile of dead ones?

A: Jab 'em all with your pitchfork.

Q: What if the live one's at the bottom?

A: Don't worry, it'll try to eat its way out.

Q: What's the problem with that?

A: If it makes it, it'll want seconds.

Q: That's disgusting, how do you stop it?

A: With your pitchfork, stupid.

A little boy asked his mother, "Do people go to heaven feet first?"

His mother replied, "Why, no. Why do you ask?"

The boy replies, "Well, the maid was lying on the bed with her feet up, hollering, "Oh God, I'm coming! And she would have, too, if Daddy hadn't held her down."

What do you call two men with no arms and no legs, hanging on the wall by the window?

Curt and Rod.

What do you call a guy in a field with no arms or legs?

Home Plate.

What do you call an armless man hanging on a wall?

Art.

What do you call an armless man floating in the water?

Bob.

What do you call an armless man lying on the ground?

Matt.

What do you call an armless woman with a sore neck?

Sue.

What do you call an armless woman with one leg?

Eileen.

What do you call an armless Japanese woman with one leg?

Irene.

What do you call an armless man with one leg?

Skip.

What do you call an armless man standing in a hole?

Doug.

What do you call an armless man with no legs?

Neal.

What do you call an armless man sitting in a pasture?

Chip.

What do you call an armless man at a bank?

Rob.

What do you call an armless man standing on a stage?

Mike.

What do you call an armless man sitting on a pot?

Stew.

What do you call a bald-headed, armless man?

Dick.

What do you call a woman with no arms or legs, cooking on a grill?

Patty.

What do you call a man with no arms or legs, flying over a fence?

Homer.

What do you call a man with no arms or legs in a pile of leaves?

Russell.

What do you call a man with no arms or legs in a hole?

Phil.

What do you call a man with no arms or legs in the mailbox?

Bill.

A drunk man was walking on the street with one foot on the curb and one foot in the gutter. A cop stopped him and said: "I've got to take you in, you're too drunk to take care of yourself."

The drunk man asked, "Officer, are you absolutely sure I am drunk?"

The officer answered, "Buddy, you're wasted."

The drunk man replied, "Thank goodness. I thought I was a cripple!"

Why are blonde jokes so short?

So men can remember them.

How do you measure a blonde's intelligence?

Stick a tire-pressure gauge in her ear.

How do you get a blonde pregnant?

Come in her shoes and let the flies do the rest.

How do you get a blonde off of your knees?

Come.

How does a blonde hold her liquor?

By the ears.

How do you know a blonde likes you?

She screws you two nights in a row.

How do you know a blonde has just lost her virginity?

Her crayons are still sticky.

How does a blonde moon walk?

She pulls down her panties and slides her ass along the floor.

Why are only 2% of blondes touch typists?

The rest are hunt'n peckers.

What nickname is most used by blondes in order to boost their popularity?

B.J.

Why are blonde's coffins Y-shaped?

Because as soon as they are on their backs, their legs open.

Why do blondes get confused in the ladies' room?

They have to pull their own pants down.

Why do blondes wear panties?

To keep their ankles warm.

What's the mating call of the blonde?

"I'm sooooo drunk!"

What is the mating call of the ugly blonde?

"I said: I'M SOOOO DRUNK!"

What's the mating call of the brunette?

When is that blond bitch going to leave!?

What's the mating call of the redhead?

"Next!"

What is the blonde doing when she holds her hands tightly over her ears?

Trying to hold on to a thought.

Why did the blonde stare at a frozen orange juice can for two hours?

Because it said 'concentrate.'

What's the difference between a blonde and an ironing board?

It's difficult to open the legs of an ironing board.

What's the difference between a blonde and a brick?

When you lay a brick it doesn't follow you around for two weeks whining.

What's the difference between a blonde and a phone booth?

You need a quarter to use the phone.

What do the Bermuda Triangle and blondes have in common?

They've both swallowed a lot of semen.

Why did God make blondes a little smarter than horses?

Because he didn't want them shitting in the streets during parades.

How does the blond turn on the light after she has had sex?

She opens the car door.

How does a blonde part her hair?

She spreads her legs.

How do you get a blonde's eyes to twinkle?

Shine a flashlight in her ears.

How do you tell when a blonde reaches orgasm?

The batteries are dead.

How do you drown a blond?

Put a mirror at the bottom of the pool.

How do you tell if a blonde did your landscaping?

The bushes are darker than the rest of the yard.

How do you describe a blonde surrounded by drooling idiots?

Flattered.

What do you call a blonde with ESP and PMS?

A know-it-all bitch.

What's the difference between a counterfeit dollar and skinny blonde?

One's a phony buck and the other is a bony fuck.

What's the difference between a chorus line of blondes and a magician?

A magician has a cunning array of stunts.

What is the best blonde secretary in the world to have?

One that never misses a period.

What's the difference between having sex with a blonde and eating Jell-O?

Jell-O wiggles when you eat it.

What two things in the air can get a blonde pregnant?

Her feet!

What's the disease that paralyzes blondes below the waist?

Marriage.

Why do blondes hate M&Ms?

They're too hard to peel.

Why did she get fired from the M&M factory?

For throwing out all the Ws.

Why don't blondes like making Kool-Aid?

Because they can't fit eight cups of water in the little packet.

How can you tell a blonde had a bad day?

Her tampon is behind her ear and she doesn't know what she did with her last cigarette.

What does a blonde say after multiple orgasms?

Way to go, team!

How can you tell if a blonde has a vibrator?

Her teeth are chipped.

How do you keep a blonde busy?

Write 'Please turn over' on both sides of a piece of paper.

Why do blondes have vaginas?

So guys will talk to them at parties.

What do you call a blonde with a runny nose?

Full.

How did the blonde break her leg playing hockey with the Maple Leaves?

She fell out of the tree.

What do you call a blonde without an asshole?

Divorced.

How is a blonde like a postage stamp?

You lick 'em, stick 'em, and send 'em on their way.

How did the blonde die drinking milk?

She was sucking so hard the cow fell on her.

How did the blonde burn her nose?

Bobbing for french fries.

How can you tell if a blonde's been using the computer?

There's Wite-Out on the screen.

Six

Gross, Gross, Gross

A woman was lying in her hospital bed, recuperating after an intense and difficult twelve-hour delivery. Suddenly, the door opened, and in walked the delivery nurse carrying her baby. The woman reaches out for her child, but the nurse throws the baby on the floor, kicks it up against the wall, picks it up, and twirls it around several times and bashes it against the wall.

The woman shouts hysterically, "What are you doing to my baby?"

The nurse starts to laugh loudly, and throws the baby out the window.

"Hey, I was just playing around," she says, "This kid's already dead."

Two statues were standing in the same town square in Greece for centuries. One was a handsome nude male, while the other was a beautiful nude female. For centuries, they had braved the cold weather and the scorching sun. One day, an angel who was flying over the city saw the two statues. He was overcome with sorrow for the two and brought them to life.

The angel said, "My powers can grant you life for one single hour. Make the most of it!"

As soon as the angel disappeared, the two smiled at each other and immediately jumped behind a nearby bush. For nearly fifty five minutes, there was a lot of noise, disturbance, screams, leaves, and feathers flying around from behind the bush.

At the end of fifty-five minutes, the man said, "Well, we have just five minutes left. What else should we do?"

"Something more of the same would be divine." said the woman.

"All right," said the man "Only this time you hold the pigeons and let me shit on them!"

A Texan, a Mexican, a Frenchman, and an Englishman are on a plane that is going to crash. The problem is, they've only got one parachute.

The Englishman flings open the door, hollers, "Long live the Queen!" and jumps to his death.

Not to be outdone by a limey bastard, the Frenchman shouts, "Viva la France!" and jumps.

Next guy up is the Texan, who shouts, "Remember the Alamo!" and throws the Mexican out.

Fred was an alcoholic. He lost his business, his wife, and family through a messy divorce, and it was all because of booze. A friend of his decided to help him, and took him to a movie theater where they were showing an old classic about an alcoholic.

As Fred watched the main character lying, cheating, stealing, and finally ending up in a straitjacket because of the booze. He began to perspire, undid his collar, mopped his face, and showed signs of extreme distress.

When the film was over and they went outside, Fred hugged his friend and said, "Thanks man, I've learned the most important lesson of my life."

"That's great," his friend cried.

"Yeah, I'm never going to the movies again."

So, Mickey Mouse was arrested for beating his wife, Minnie.

At the trial, the judge said, "Now Mickey, I understand that you said Minnie was acting very silly recently. But surely that doesn't give you the right to hit her."

"But your honor," said Mickey, "I didn't say she was acting silly. I said she was fucking Goofy!"

Snow White and the Seven Dwarfs are in Rome for a tour of the city. One night Grumpy doesn't come back to the hotel, and he's in a very bad mood. Snow White tries to cheer him up, but Grumpy is very upset and, after a few days, his mood still hasn't improved. He falls into a deep depression and says the only person on earth who can help him is the Pope. So, Snow White arranges a meeting with the Pope at the Vatican to try and help him out. The dwarfs wait outside while Grumpy has his audience.

"Your Holiness, do you have any really short nuns?" asks Grumpy.

"No, my son, all our nuns are at least five feet tall."

"Are you sure? I mean, you wouldn't have any nuns that are, say, about my height? Maybe a little shorter?"

"I'm afraid not. Why do you ask?"

"Positive? Nobody in a habit that's about two and a half feet tall?"

"I'm sure, Grumpy, my son."

"Okay." Grumpy seems really upset, and the Pope wonders why. So he listens to the dwarfs as they leave the building.

"What'd he say? What'd he say?" shouted his friends.

Grumpy says, "He said they don't have any."

And they all started chanting, "Grumpy fucked a penguin! Grumpy fucked a penguin! Grumpy fucked a penguin!"

Q: How many real men does it take to change a lightbulb?

A: None, real men aren't afraid of the dark.

Q: How many real women does it take to change a light-bulb?

A: None, real women have plenty of real men to do it for them.

Q: How many folk singers does it take to change a light-bulb?

A: Two, one to change to bulb, and the other to write a song about how good the old lightbulb was.

Q: How many policemen does it take to screw a lightbulb?

A: None, the fucking lightbulb better turn itself in—if it knows what's good for it.

Q: How many conservative economists does it take to change a lightbulb?

A: None, if the government leaves it alone, the darkness will improve by itself.

Q: How many mystery writers does it take to change a lightbulb?

A: Only one, but it needs a spectacular twist at the end.

Q: How many secret policemen does it take to change a lightbulb?

A: There never was a bad lightbulb, why would YOU suggest there was?

There's this golfer who usually has a nasty slice but during this particular round, he's overcompensating and hooking badly off the tee. After much searching of the rough on the left of the fairway, he finally locates his ball sitting in the middle of a bed of buttercups. Well, he thinks, they're beautiful but I gotta play it where it lies. He starts whacking away. The buttercups are flying, and suddenly there's a clap of thunder and a brilliant flash of light, and a woman appears before him dressed in a filmy white gown.

"Who are you?" the man asks.

"I'm mother nature," the woman says, "I've seen what you've done to my buttercups and now you're going to pay. For one year, you can have no butter. I have spoken."

"Whew," he says, wiping his forehead, "that's a relief."

"Didn't you hear me, mister?" mother nature says, "No butter for a year."

"Lady, you don't understand," the man replies. "Today I hooked, usually I slice. If I played like normal, the ball would be over on the other side of the fairway in that clump of pussy willows."

A young man went to pick up his date at her apartment. She wasn't quite ready and handed him a red rubber ball, suggesting he play with her dog while he waited. The dog was loving it, but the man got bored and started tossing the ball farther and farther away, into the kitchen and behind the couch, just to keep the dog busy.

The dog never seemed to get tired, and the man was getting irritated, so finally he tossed the ball as hard as he could and it bounced off a barstool and onto the balcony. The dog leapt in the air, caught the ball in his mouth, and went sailing over the balcony rail. The problem was the man's date lived on the nineteenth floor.

Just as he was about to look over the edge, his date bounced into the room, excited and ready to go. He knew she really liked him. They were in the elevator by the time he could even think to say anything. But it was too late, the moment had passed, so he said nothing. He was distant during dinner, terribly distracted. He couldn't pay attention at the movies. During the cab ride back, he was in a state of panic.

What was he going to say? How was he going to tell her?

As she put her keys into the lock, he turned to her and said, "You know, your dog looked sort of depressed."

Ed was devoted to his cat. He had special cat toys, special foods, special litter. Everything a cat could require, Ed provided. When he had to be out of town on business for a month, and knew he couldn't take Tabitha with him, he called on his younger brother. George agreed to watch Tabitha, to brush her, to feed her, to change the litter at the right intervals. Ed made him promise to spend time with Tabitha so that she wouldn't get lonely. Ed went on his business trip, certain that Tabitha was in good hands. He called the first night to see how things were going.

"How's Tabitha?" he asked George.

"The cat's dead!" was George's only reply.

Ed was stunned.

"George, you know what Tabitha meant to me. You didn't have to be that abrupt. You could have broken it to me gently. You could have said, 'Tabitha is up on the roof. Don't worry. We'll get her down.' Then, you could have told me that Tabitha was at the vet's but that he was confident she'd be OK. Then, the next time I called you could have broken it to me that she'd passed away. Do you see what I mean?"

"I guess so," George conceded, "I could have been gentler I guess."

"Good. I feel better getting that off my chest. How's Mom?"

"Mom's up on the roof," George confided.

Why are chickens so ugly?

You would be too if you have a pecker hanging out of your forehead.

What's green and smells like pork?

Kermit's middle finger.

What's the brown stuff between elephants' toes?

Slow natives.

What do you get when you cross a donkey with an onion?

A piece of ass that makes your eyes water.

How do you say "fuck you" in Hollywood?

"Trust me."

Why do dogs lick their balls?

Because they can.

What is organic dental floss?

Pubic hair.

Why is there a string on the end of a tampon?

So men can floss after they eat.

How do you get four queers on a barstool?

Turn it upside down.

Did you hear about the queer nail?

He lay in the road and blew a tire.

Where are an elephant's genitals?

In his feet . . . If he steps on you, you're fucked.

Why does Hillary Clinton always climb on top?

Because Bill can only fuck up.

Why does Miss Piggy use a honey-and-vinegar douche?

Because Kermit likes sweet and sour pork.

Why is being a dick not all it's cracked up to be?

First of all, you have a head but no brains, there are a couple of nuts following you around all the time, your next door neighbor is an asshole, and your best friend is a cunt.

Two beautiful Swedish housemaids are having their pictures taken.

The first one asks, "Why is he looking at us like that?"

The second replies, "He's got to focus."

"Oh, no," says the first one, "You tell him he has to take the picture first."

A man takes a girl out in his car, stops seven miles out of town, and says he wants to fuck her. She refuses and walks back. The second night, he takes her twelve miles out of town and tells her he really wants to fuck her. She refuses and walks back. The third night, he takes her thirty miles away, and lo and behold, she gives in.

Afterwards he asks why she finally gave in.

She shrugged, "I'll walk seven miles, or even twelve miles, to save a friend of mine from a case of AIDS. But not thirty, no way."

A man arrives at the gates of heaven.

St. Peter asks, "Religion?"

The man says, "Episcopalian."

St. Peter looks down his list, and says, "Go to room twenty-four. But be very quiet as you pass room eight."

Another man arrives at the gates of heaven.

"Religion?"

"Baptist."

Go to room eighteen. But be very quiet as you pass room eight."

A third man arrives at the gates.

"Religion?"

"Jewish."

"Go to room eleven. But be very quiet as you pass room eight."

The man says, "I can understand there being different rooms for different religions, but why do I have to be quiet when I pass room eight?"

St. Peter shrugs, "Well the Catholics are in room eight, and they think they're the only ones here."

A woman of thirty-five thinks of having children. What does a man of thirty-five think of?

Dating children.

How can you tell soap operas are fictional?

In real life, men aren't affectionate after they get laid.

What should you give a man who has everything?

A woman to show him how to work it.

Why do black widow spiders kill their males after mating?

To stop the snoring before it starts.

Why don't most men have midlife crises?

They're stuck in adolescence.

How was Colonel Sanders a typical male?

All he cared about were legs, breasts, and thighs.

How is being at a singles bar different from going to the circus?

At the circus the clowns don't talk.

What makes men chase women they have no intention of marrying?

The same urge that makes dogs chase cars they have no intention of driving.

What do you do with a bachelor who thinks he's God's gift?

Exchange him.

Why do bachelors like smart women?

Opposites attract.

Why are husbands like lawn mowers?

They're hard to get started, emit foul odors, and don't work, half the time.

What's the difference between a new husband and a new dog?

After a year, the dog is still excited to see you.

Why is sleeping with a man like a soap opera?

Just when it's getting interesting, they're finished until next time.

Why do men find it difficult to make eye contact?

Breasts don't have eyes.

How many men does it take to screw in a lightbulb?

One. Men will screw anything!

What's a man's idea of foreplay?

A half hour of begging.

How can you tell if a man is sexually excited?

He's breathing.

What's the difference between men and government bonds?

Bonds mature.

What do men and beer bottles have in common?

They're both empty from the neck up.

How many men does it take to change a roll of toilet paper?

We don't know—it's never happened.

A couple of drunks are sitting at a bar on the tenth story of a building.

The first one says, "See that window over there? Well, if you were to jump out that window, the air pressure rising from the street would keep you from hitting the ground. In fact, not only won't you hit the ground, but you'll also fly back up to the window."

The second drunk says, "You're full of shit! You think I'm nuts?"

The first drunk says, "OK. I'll show you."

He goes over to the window and jumps out. Seconds later, he rises back up to the window ledge and comes back in the bar.

"See? Now you try it. It's fun."

The second drunk can't believe it. He reaches over and pats his friend to make sure he's real. Then he says to the bartender, "By God, he's right. I'm gonna do it!" He walks over to the window, climbs out on the ledge, and jumps. As soon as he's falling, he starts screaming.

Just as he hits the ground ten stories below, the bartender turns to the man and says, "Clark Kent, you are one mean son of a bitch."

Two drunks are sitting at a bar, getting wasted. There's a dog over in the corner licking and licking his balls in a frenzy.

The first drunk points to the dog and says, "Boy, I sure wish I could do that."

And the second drunk says, "I bet if you ask real nice, he'd let you."

An old man was taking a walk in the park and spied an attractive old lady sitting on a park bench.

He asked her, "Can you guess my age?"

She replied, "Yes, but first you will have to take off all your clothes." The old man was proud of his physique, so he agreed.

"OK, that's done. Now, can you guess my age?"

"Yes," she responded, "but now I want you to dance around a little for me." The old man was sure of his strength, so he consented.

"OK, that's enough. Now can you guess my age?"

She guessed, "Well, I would say you are three months shy of your eighty-fifth birthday."

"Wow, you're right—but how did you know that?" he asked.

She answered, "You told me yesterday, but I wanted to see what you looked like without any clothes on."

Seven

Gross Homosexual Jokes

A guy dies and finds himself in hell and has his first meeting with a demon.

Demon: Why so glum, chum?

Guy: Why do you think? I'm in hell.

Demon: Hell's not so bad. We actually have a lot of fun down here. You a drinkin' man?

Guy: Sure, I love to drink.

Demon: Well, you're gonna love Mondays, then. On Mondays, that's all we do is drink. Whiskey, tequila, Guinness, wine coolers, diet Tab . . . We drink till we throw up, and then we drink some more.

Guy: Gee, that sounds great.

Demon: You a smoker?

Guy: You better believe it.

Demon: All right! You're gonna love Tuesdays. We get the finest cigars from around the world and smoke our lungs out. If you get cancer, it's okay . . . you're already dead.

Guy: No shit!

Demon: I bet you like to gamble.

Guy: Yes, as a matter of fact I do.

Demon: Good, because Wednesday is gambling day. Craps, blackjack, horse races, you name it. We even opened up a pai gow poker table.

Guy: Hmmm, I never played pai gow before. . . .

Demon: Well, now you can. You like to do drugs?

Guy: Yes, I love to do drugs. You don't mean. . . .

Demon: That's right! Thursday is drug day. Help yourself to a great big bowl of crack. Smoke a doobie the size of a submarine. You can do all the drugs you want, and if you overdose, it's okay . . . You're already dead.

Guy: Wow! I never realized that hell was such a swingin' place!

Demon: You gay?

Guy: Uh, no.

Demon: Oooh, you're gonna hate Fridays.

Why do faggots love bakeries?

There are plenty of fresh buns in the back.

What's a lesbian's favorite perfume?

U'de Tuna.

Why did the bull dyke use cigars when she got her period?

She thought tampons were for faggots and anyway, you couldn't smoke'em when you were done.

Q. What do Michael Jackson and KMart have in common?

A. Little boys' underwear half off.

Q. How do you know when it's time for bed at the Jackson home.

A. When the big hand touches the little hand.

What's the difference between a priest and a fag?

Not much.

How can you tell a really butch lesbian?

She jump-starts her dildo and her pussy smells like a truck because she douches with diesel fuel.

A man walks into a public bathroom and begins using one of the urinals. He looks to his left and sees a very short man also peeing. Suddenly, the short man looks up at the taller man, and the taller man is completely embarrassed about staring at the smaller man's penis.

"Sorry," says the taller man. "I'm not gay or anything, but you have the longest penis I've ever seen, especially on a man so small!"

"Well," says the leprechaun, "That's because I'm a leprechaun! All leprechauns have dicks this size!"

The taller man says, "Incredible! I'd give anything if mine were that long."

"Well, what with me being a leprechaun and all, I can make your wish come true. All you have to do is let me take you into that stall over there and fuck you."

"Well," says the man, "I don't know about that, but . . . OK!"

"Say," says the leprechaun while he pumps the man in the butt, "How old are you, son?"

"Thirty-two," grunts the man.

"Imagine that," says the little man, "Thirty-two and you still believe in leprechauns!"

Why was the gay politician confused?

He kept wanting to kiss hands and shake babies.

What do you call a gay bar with no place to sit?

A fruit stand.

What did one lesbian say to the other?

Let me be Frank with you.

What's the sign hanging in the gay cafeteria?

First Cum, First Served.

Why did a gay guy get a job at the heating company?

He liked it in the coal chute.

Did you hear about the gay father who liked his baby's asshole so much that he had it bronzed as a memento?

Why didn't the cop believe the gay burglar?

Somehow he knew that the kid wasn't cuming clean.

Why did the faggot get a job at the loading dock?

He loved taking deliveries in the rear.

Why did the queer get fired from the German restaurant?

His sausage kept getting hard in the kitchen.

Why did the lesbian come back from France?

She missed her native tongue.

Did you hear about the queer in the castle's livery stable?

He went down for the Count.

How can you tell a sadistic, animal-hating lesbian?

She's always hitting beavers with sticks.

Three lesbians were talking in a bar. One of them was Polish.

"I love pussy, it's so warm and furry." the first one said.

"I love pussy, too, it's so sweet and soft. I just love to kiss it," said the second.

"I love it, too," said the Polish one, "but how do you keep it from scratching you when you fuck it."

How can you tell a gay baseball player?

He loves to put his bat on your balls.

Why did the dykes rush the new bakery?

They heard everything was made from dill-dough.

Why do gay golfers love playing in Puerto Rico?

Everyday they get to try for another hole in Juan.

What's impossible to see and smells like cum?

Faggot farts.

Why were the two faggots disappointed in their trip to Mexico?

They thought they were going to see some real cock-fighting.

Why was the faggot thrown out off the softball team?

He kept thinking they were saying butter up.

Why can't gays play the outfield?

All they want to do is drop flys.

Why do faggots make great linemen?

They love to penetrate the defense.

Why couldn't the gay quarterback make it in the NFL?

He never wanted to come out of the huddle.

What's another reason the gay quarterback couldn't make it in the NFL?

Every time the linemen bent over he got a boner.

And what's another reason the gay quarterback couldn't make it in the NFL?

He was too forward with his passes.

Why couldn't the Polish faggot make a living as a hooker?

He didn't understand that blow was just an expression.

Did you hear about the faggot cop?

He always got his man in the end.

Did you hear how they finally got the lesbian anorexics to eat?

They put pussy hair around the dinner plates.

Why did they fire the faggot cop?

He kept blowing his cases.

Why did they fire the other faggot cop?

He was a sucker for men in uniform.

How can you tell a really tough dyke?

She rolls her tampons out of burlap.

What's a huge fart in a men's room in a bus station?

A faggot love call.

Why did the gay crook keep going back to jail?

He just loved it in the can.

What do you call it when a gay politician fucks his assistant?

A congressional probe.

Why did the closet congressman want to question gays in the military?

He looked forward to some penetrating examinations.

Did you hear about the gay Polish bank robber?

He tied up the safe and blew the tellers.

What's an event queens would like to see added to the Olympics?

Drag racing.

Why was the hairdresser fired from the Richard Simmon's infomercial?

He kept rubbing Dick in public.

How do you know you're in a lesbian bar?

There are no balls on the pool table and all the cues are sticky.

Eight

Nasty Sex Jokes

There was this bar in need of a piano player, so the manager hung a "Piano Player Wanted" sign in the window. An hour or so later, a man walked in and asked to audition. The manager says, "Go ahead and play something." The man sits down and begins to play the greatest music the manager has ever heard. Tears are welling up in his eyes as the man ends the song. The manager tells the man that that's the best thing he's ever heard and asks for the name of the song.

The man says, "I wrote that song. I call it 'Two Queers Taking it in the Ass.' "

The manager winces, but before he can say anything the man starts to play an even more beautiful song. This time, when he ends the manager is weeping. Wiping away a tear, he tells the man that that's the loveliest song he's ever heard.

The man says, "I wrote that song too. I call it 'Six Guys Doing one Really Fat Chick.' "

The manager winces again but comes to a solution. He tells the man the job is his, but he can't tell the customers the names of the songs. The man understands and agrees to start the next night at 9:00 P.M. At 9:05 he comes charging through the door with his tux shirt unbuttoned, his fly open, and his dick sticking out of his pants. He races over to the piano and proceeds to play the most beautiful music anyone has ever heard.

The manager calls one of his waitresses over and tells her to tell the man that his fly is down and his dick is sticking out of his pants. The waitress makes her way over to the man and whispers in his ear, "Do you know your fly is down and your dick is sticking out of your pants?"

The man replies, "Know it? I wrote it!"

One day, while on patrol, a police officer pulled a car over for speeding. He went up to the car and asked the driver to roll down her window.

The first thing he noticed, besides the nice red sports car, was how hot the driver was! A drop-dead gorgeous blonde, the works.

"I've pulled you over for speeding, ma'am. . . . Could I see your driver's license. . . ."

"License? . . ." replied the blonde, instantly revealing that she was dumb as a stump.

"It's usually in your wallet. . . ." replied the officer.

Alter fumbling for a few minutes, the blonde managed to find it.

"Now may I see your registration. . . ." asked the cop.

"Registration . . . what's that? . . ." asked the blonde.

"It's usually in your glove compartment . . ." said the cop impatiently.

After more fumbling, she found the registration.

"I'll be back in a minute," said the cop and walked back to his car.

The officer radioed the dispatch to run a check on the

woman's license and registration. After a few moments, the dispatcher came back.

"Ummm . . . is this woman driving a red sports car?"

"Yes," replied the officer.

"Is she a drop-dead gorgeous blonde?" asked the dispatcher.

"Uh . . . yes" replied the cop.

"Here's what you do. . . ." said the dispatcher. "Give her the stuff back, and drop your pants . . ."

"I can't do that. That's crazy!" exclaimed the cop.

"Trust me . . . just do it. . . ." said the dispatcher.

So the cop returned to the blonde, gave back the license and registration, and dropped his pants just like the dispatcher said.

The blonde looked down and sighed, "Oh no . . . not ANOTHER breathalyzer. . . ."

A sixty-year-old woman came home one day and heard strange noises in her bedroom. She opened the door and discovered her forty-year-old daughter playing with a vibrator. "What are you doing?" asked the mom.

"Mom, I am forty years old and look at me. I am ugly. I will never get married, so this is pretty much my husband." The mother walked out of the room, shaking her head.

The next day the father came home and heard noises in the bedroom, and, upon entering the room, found his daughter using the vibrator.

"What the hell are you doing?" he asked.

His daughter replied, "I already told Mom; I am forty years old now and ugly. I will never get married, so this is as close as I'll ever get to a husband." The father walked out of the room shaking his head, too.

The next day the mother came home to find her husband with a beer in one hand and the vibrator sitting next to him as he watched the football game.

"For Christ's sake, what are you doing?" she cried. The husband replied, "What does it look like I'm doing? I'm having a beer and watching the game with my new son-in-law!"

A young man goes into a drugstore to buy condoms. The pharmacist says the condoms come in packs of 3, 9, or 12, and asks which the young man wants.

"Well," he said, "I've been seeing this girl for a while and she's really hot. I want the condoms because I think tonight's *the* night. We're having dinner with her parents, and then we're going out. And I've got a feeling I'm gonna get lucky after that. Once she's had me, she'll want me all the time, so you'd better give me the 12-pack."

The young man makes his purchase and leaves. Later that evening, he sits down to dinner with his girlfriend and her parents. He asks if he might give the blessing, and they agree. He begins the prayer, but continues praying for several minutes.

The girl leans over and says, "You never told me that you were such a religious person."

He leans over to her and says, "You never told me that your father is a pharmacist."

A very handsome young man lost his eye in a car accident. His doctor told him he could get a glass replacement that would be almost perfect. But it cost a lot more than the young man could afford.

"Well," the doctor said, "Until you can afford a glass eye, I'll make you one made of wood. It won't look as good, but it's a lot cheaper." The man agrees and gets fitted for the wooden eye. But it looks exactly like what it is—wood—and he becomes so self-conscious about it that he stops going out of his house.

One Saturday night, his friends finally convince him to go out to a bar with them. He's reluctant, but he goes. Everybody is dancing and drinking and having a great time, and he's feeling more and more lonely, and he was just about to leave when he sees a girl standing over in the corner.

He edges his way toward her and sees that she's got this horrible harelip and is also hunchbacked. "Perfect," he figures, "This girl is so much worse off than me that she can't possibly turn me down."

He goes up to her and says timidly, "Wanna dance?"

The girl is really surprised and says excitedly, "Would I. . . ."

The guy flips out, "Wood eye! Wood eye! Well, fuck you, you hunchbacked, fucking harelip!"

Leroy was telling his friend Bubba about the date he had the night before. "It was a bummer. She used four-letter words all evening." Bubba exclaimed, "Really? I can't believe you didn't enjoy that." "Guess again," said Leroy, "All night she kept saying 'Quit,' 'Stop,' and 'Don't!' "

A businessman and his secretary are really hot for each other, and the exec convinces her to come to his place for a quickie. "Don't worry," he whispered, "My wife is out of town on a business trip."

They start to get it on when the secretary gasps, "We got to stop now! I'm not using any birth control."

"No problem" he stutters, "I know where my wife keeps her diaphragm. . . ."

He heads to the bathroom and is gone for quite a while. The secretary gets bored and calls out, "What's the problem, sweetie?"

He storms into the bedroom empty-handed. "That bitch!" he shouts, "She took it with her! I always knew she didn't trust me. . . ."

Three friends were sitting around one day talking about their husbands, and they decided to give them nicknames because they were all named Rufus, and they were getting confused about who was talking about whom. After a little discussion, they decided to name their men after different sodas.

The first woman said, "I'm gonna call my man 'Mountain Dew.'

"Why?" the others asked.

"Because he's big as a mountain, and he wants to do it all the time."

The second woman thinks for a minute, and says, "I'm gonna call my Rufus "Seven Up."

"Why?" the others asked.

"Because he got seven inches and they're always up."

"What about you, baby?" the women ask their last friend.

The woman thinks and thinks and then says, "Why, hell, I think I call him Mr. Jack Daniels."

"You breakin' the rules," the other women shouted. "Jack Daniels ain't no soda, it's a hard liquor."

"I knows that," she smiled, "so's my Rufus."

A new priest at his first mass was so nervous he could hardly speak. After mass, he asked the monsignor how he had done.

The monsignor said that he didn't do very well, but went on to say, "When I'm worried about getting nervous on the pulpit, I put a glass of vodka next to the water glass. If I start to get nervous, I take a sip."

So, the next Sunday, he took the monsignor's advice. At the beginning of the sermon, he got nervous and took a drink and then another. Afterward, he was certain he had given the best sermon of his life.

Upon returning to his office after mass, he found the following list nailed to his door:

For Your Information, Father—

1. There are ten commandments, not twelve, and there are twelve disciples, not ten.
2. Jesus was consecrated, not "constipated."
3. Jacob wagered his donkey, he did not "bet his ass."
4. We do not refer to Jesus Christ as "the late J.C."
5. The Father, Son, and Holy Ghost are not referred to as "Daddy, Junior, and the Spook."
6. David slew Goliath, he did not "kick the shit out of him."
7. David was hit by a rock and knocked off his donkey, he wasn't "stoned off his ass."
8. We do not refer to the holy cross as "big Mr. T."
9. When Jesus broke bread at the Last Supper he said, "Take this and eat, for it is my body." He did not say, "Eat me up, baby."
10. The Virgin Mary is not referred to as "Cherry Mary."
11. Next Sunday there will be a taffy-pulling contest at St. Peter's, not a "peter-pulling contest at St. Taffy's."
12. Sip the goddamned Vodka, don't gulp.

Nine
Totally Disgusting and Silly Lists

CONFUCIUS SAY:

1. Woman who goes to man's apartment for snack, gets titbit.
2. Man who lay woman on ground, get peace on earth.
3. Man who gets kicked in testicles, left holding the bag.
4. Man who kisses girl's behind, gets crack in face.
5. Passionate kiss like spiderweb—lead to undoing of fly.
6. Man with holes in pockets, feels cocky all day.
7. Man who fight with wife all day, get no piece at night.
8. Virginity like balloon—one prick, all gone.
9. Girl who rides bicycle, peddles ass all over town.
10. He who farts in church, sit in own pew.
11. Baseball all wrong—man with four balls can't walk.
12. Man who live in glass house, dress in basement.
13. Kotex not best thing on earth, but next-to-best thing.
14. Man with penis in peanut butter jar is fucking nuts.

15. Man who walk through airport door sideways is going to Bangkok.

16. Man who drop watch in toilet, bound to have shitty time.

17. Man who take lady on camping trip, have one intent.

WHICH BRAND OF CONDOM FITS YOU THE BEST?

AT&T Condoms: "Reach out and touch someone!!!"
Avis Condoms: Trying harder than ever!!!
Bounty Condoms: The quicker picker-upper!!!
California Lotto Condoms: Who's next!!!
Campbell's Soup Condoms: Mm, mm good!!!
Chevron Condoms: Use them? People do!!!
Chevy Condoms: Like a rock!!!
Coca Cola Condoms: Always a Real Thing!!!
Delta Airlines Travel Pack Condoms: Delta's ready when you are!!!
Dial Condoms: Aren't you glad you use it? Don't you wish everybody did?
Diet Pepsi Condoms: You got the right one, baby!!!
Double Mint Condom: Double your pleasure, double your fun!!!
Energizer Condom: It keeps going and going and going!!!
Flintstones Vitamins Condom Pack: Ten million strong and growing!!!
Ford Condoms: The best never rest!!!
General Electric Condoms: We bring good things to life!!!
KFC Condoms: Finger-Licking Good!!!
Lays Condoms: Betcha can't have just one!!!
M&Ms Condom: "It melts in your mouth, not in your hands!!!"
Macintosh Condoms: It does more, it costs less, its that simple!!!
MCI Condoms: For friends and family!!!
Mentos Condoms: The freshmaker!!!
Microsoft Condoms: Where do you want to go today?
New York Lotto Condoms: 'Cause, hey—you never know!!!

Nike Condoms: Just do it!!!

Pringles Condoms: Once you pop, you can't stop!!!

Secret Condoms: Strong enough for a man, but Ph balanced for a woman!!!

Taco Bell Condom: Get some; make a run for the border!!!

The Carl Jr. Condom: If it don't get all over the place, it doesn't belong in your face. . . .

The Sears Latex condom: One coat is good for the entire winter!!!

The Star Trek Condom: To Boldly Go Where No Man Has Gone Before!!!

Toyota Condoms: Oh what a feeling!!!!

United Airlines Travel Pack Condoms: Fly United!!!

THINK ABOUT THIS. . . .

One week before Lincoln's death, he was in Monroe, Maryland.

One week before Kennedy's death, he was in Marilyn Monroe.

TOP TEN REASONS WHY BEER IS BETTER THAN JESUS

10. No one will kill you for not drinking Beer.
9. Beer doesn't tell you how to have sex.
8. Beer has never caused a major war.
7. They don't force Beer on minors who can't think for themselves.
6. When you have a Beer, you don't knock on people's doors trying to give it away.
5. Nobody's ever been burned at the stake, hanged, or tortured over his brand of Beer.
4. You don't have to wait 2000+ years for a second Beer.
3. There are laws saying Beer labels can't lie to you.
2. You can prove you have a Beer.
1. If you've devoted your life to Beer, there are groups to help you stop.

TWENTY-FIVE REASONS WHY A BEER IS BETTER THAN A WOMAN

1. You can enjoy a Beer anytime of the month.
2. Beer stains wash out.
3. You don't have to wine and dine Beer.
4. Your Beer will always wait patiently for you in the car while you play football with the guys.
5. When a Beer is flat you toss it out.
6. Beer is never late.
7. Hangovers go away!
8. A Beer doesn't get jealous when you grab another Beer.
9. Beer labels come off without a fight.
10. When you go to a bar you know you can always pick up a Beer.
11. Beer never has a headache.
12. After you've had a Beer, the bottle is still worth ten cents.
13. A Beer won't get upset if you come home with another Beer on your breath.
14. If you pour a Beer right, you'll always get good head.
15. You can have more than one Beer in a night and not feel guilty.
16. A Beer always goes down easy.
17. You can share a Beer with your friends.
18. You always know you're the first one to pop a Beer.
19. Beer is always wet.
20. Beer doesn't demand equality.
21. You can have a Beer in public.
22. A Beer doesn't care when you cum.
23. A frigid Beer is a good Beer.
24. You don't have to wash a Beer before it tastes good.
25. If you change Beers, you won't have to pay alimony.

IF COCKS WERE CLASSIFIED BY BRAND NAMES

All-State Penis: You're in good hands.

American Express Penis: Don't leave home without it.

Army Penis: Be all that you can be.

AT&T Penis: Reach out and touch someone.

Bacardi Penis: Taste the feeling.

Beef Penis: It's what's for dinner.

Borden Penis: It's GOT to be good.

Bounce Penis: With Static-Guard!

Bud-Lite Penis: Great taste, less filling.

Budweiser Penis: This bud's for you.

Burger King Penis: Have it your way.

Charmin Penis: Don't squeeze the Penis!

Chevy Truck Penis: Like a rock!

Citibank-Visa Penis: It's everywhere you want to be.

Crest Penis: Recommended by three out of four dentists.

Diet-Coke Penis: Just for the taste of it. . . .

Diet-Pepsi Penis: Uh-huh.

Doublemint Penis: Chewing really satisfies.

Duracell Penis: The copper-top Penis.

Ego Penis: Leggo my Penis.

Energizer Penis: It keeps going and going.

Equal Penis: Tastes like sugar.

Excedrin Penis: It's tthhhhiiiiiiissss big.

Flintstones' Vitamins Penis: Ten million strong and growing.

Folger's Crystals Penis: The best part of waking up is a Penis in your cup.

Ford Penis: Built Ford tough!

Frosted-Flakes Penis: They're GGGRRRRRREEEEAAAAATTT!

Gillette Penis: The best a man can get.

Heinz Penis: Good things come to those who wait.

Heinz Penis: Two and half inches of terror.

Jell-O Penis: Look at it wiggle, look at it jiggle.

Jewel Penis: Take a new look at an old friend.

Juicy Fruit Penis: The taste is gonna move ya.

Kentucky-Fried-Chicken Penis: Everybody needs a little KFCP.

Kix Penis: Kid-tested, mother-approved.

Life-Savers Penis: Five fruity flavors.

Little Caesar's Penis: Penis!! Penis!!

Magnavox Penis: Smart. Very smart.

Mazda Penis: It just feels right.

McDonald's Penis: Over eight billion served.

Milk Penis: It does a body good. (Got Penis?)

Mr. Clean Penis: Is it wet or is it dry?

Neon Penis: Hi.

Nintendo Penis: Now you're playing with power.

Nuprin Penis: Little, yellow, different.

NyQuil Penis: The nighttime-coughing-sneezing-runny-nose-itching-burning-so-you-can't-rest Penis.

Payday Penis: Its almost totally nuts!

Pizza Hut Penis: Makin' it great.

Pork Penis: The other white meat.

Purdue Penis: More meat, less bone.

Ragu Penis: Comes out chunkier than the rest.

Raid Penis: Kills bugs dead.

Reese's Penis: How do you eat your Reese's?

Rice Krispies Penis: What does your Penis say to you?

Right-Guard Penis: Anything less is uncivilized.

Robutussin Penis: Recommended by Dr. Mom . . .

Sanka Penis: Good to the last drop.

Sears Penis: Come see the brighter side.

Secret Penis: Strong enough for a man, but made for a woman.

The Seven-up Penis: The UN-Penis.

Snickers Penis: It satisfies you.

Sprite Penis: Image is nothing. . . . taste is everything.

Starburst Penis: The juice is loose.

Subway Penis: Where fresh is the taste.

Swiss-Miss Penis: The taste you can enjoy anytime, anywhere!

Timex Penis: Takes a lickin' and keeps on. . . .

Tombstone Penis: What would you like on your Penis?

Tootsie Roll Pop Penis: How many licks DOES it take . . . ?

Toyota Penis: I love what you do for me.

Twizzler Penis: It makes mouths happy.

U. S. Army Penis: We want *you!*

Virginia Slims Penis: You've come a long way, baby.

Windows '95 Penis: If you ask it to do too much, it'll crash.

Yellow Pages Penis: Let your fingers do the walkin.'

TOP TWENTY-FIVE-REASONS THAT HOCKEY IS BETTER THAN SEX

25. It's OK to bleed during play.

24. If it's a bad game, you can call a time-out.

23. Every player usually has two or three sticks to choose from.

22. There is a limit to the sizes of all equipment.

21. You can still play when you get married.

20. You can change on the fly.

19. Anytime you see an open net, you can go for it.

18. If you can't get it up, who cares?

17. You can score on all the teams in the league over and over again.

16. You can pull the goalie without getting yelled at.

15. It is broadcast live on TV.

14. Everyone can shoot at the same goal.

13. You can shoot in the goal and it's a good thing.

12. Because of the face-mask, nothing can get in your eyes!

11. You always know how big the stick is.

10. It's legal to play hockey professionally.

9. The puck is always hard.

8. Protective equipment is reusable, and you don't ever have to wash it.

7. It lasts a full hour.

6. You know you're finished when the buzzer sounds.

5. Your parents cheer when you score.

4. Periods only last twenty minutes.

3. You can count on it at least twice a week, four times a night.

2. You can tell your friends about it afterwards.

And, the number-one reason hockey is better than sex—A two-on-one or three-on-one is not uncommon.

TOP-TEN REASONS OJ IS SUCH AN AVID GOLFER

10. Get to wear nicely tight-fitting gloves.

9. An easy drive down the fairway which doesn't attract as much attention as an easy drive down the freeway.

8. You don't have to race home when you're finished.

7. If you say you were practicing your golf swing, people believe you immediately.

6. Slice all you want without going to jail.

5. Your driver doesn't notice if you're not there.

4. The bag is big enough to hold plenty of bloody clothing.

3. You can get caught in a lie, and no one will judge you.

2. Golf carts don't have consoles, where irritating blood smears can accumulate.

1. Get to knock around something white eighty times a day.

HOW TO KNOW IF YOU'RE A REDNECK

1. You've spray-painted your girlfriend's name on an overpass.

2. You consider a six-pack and a bug zapper quality entertainment.

3. Your lifetime goal is to own a fireworks stand.

4. When someone asks to see your I.D., you show your belt buckle.

5. Your junior and senior proms had a day care.

6. Your mother does not remove the Marlboro Light from her lips before telling the state patrolman to kiss her ass.

7. You've used lard in bed.

8. The primary color of your car is "Bondo."

9. The directions to your house include "turn off the paved road."

10. Your dog and your wallet are both on chains.

11. Your kids are going hungry tonight because you just had to have those Yosemite Sam mud flaps.

12. You owe the taxidermist more than your annual income.

13. You have lost at least one tooth opening a beer bottle.

14. Jack Daniel makes your list of most admired Americans.

15. Your wife's hairdo has been ruined by a ceiling fan.

16. You see no need for a rest stop because there's an empty milk jug in the car.

17. You have a rag for a gas cap.

18. Your dog can't watch you eat without gagging.

19. You have a Hefty bag on the passenger side front window of your car.

20. You barbecue Spam.

21. You often have to scratch your sister's name from the message "For a good time call———."

22. Your brother-in-law is also your uncle.

23. Red Man Tobacco sends you a Christmas card.

24. You bought a VCR so you could tape wrestling, while you were at work.

25. Your dad walks you to school because you're both in the same grade.

26. Your wife has a beer belly, and you find it attractive.

27. You view the upcoming family reunion as a chance to meet girls.

28. You prominently display the souvenir you got at Graceland.

29. Your house doesn't have curtains, unlike your truck.

30. When your front porch collapses, three or more dogs die.

31. You've signed a petition to change the national anthem to "Nothing Could Be Finer Than to Be in Carolina."

32. You call the boss Dude.

33. You think Volvo is part of a woman's anatomy.

34. You consider your license plate personalized because your father made it.

35. You've been fired from a construction job because of your appearance.

36. You need one more hole punched in your card to get a freebie at "The House of Tattoos."

37. Your father encouraged you to quit school because Larry had an opening on the lube rack.

38. You need an estimate from the barber before you get a haircut.

39. After making love, you ask your date to roll down the window.

A YOUNG BLACKMAN'S EBONICS DICTIONARY

Afford: "I wanted to buy a Cadillac, but then had to settle for afford."

Anus: "The policeman told me and my friend Jerome they be looking for the two guys that held up the liquor store and we said, anus, man."

Assert: "On the way home from work, I always take assert so my old lady don't smell liquor on my breath."

Bagdad: "I always wondered what was in the Bagdad use to drink out of when he was sitting on the front porch."

Battery: "The coach told my cousin Reggie he better start swinging the battery won't be in the line up tomorrow."

Beware: "I asked the man at the employment office, 'This beware I find me a job?' "

Button: "My girlfriend Juanita bought some leopard-skin stretch pants. I said girl, you won't get you button 'em."

Catacomb: "I went to the Douglas-Hollyfield fight and sat next to Don King; man, someone oughta get that catacomb."

Clothesline: "When I came home late again, I found my clothesline on the porch."

Coatroom: "The judge said, 'One more outburst like that and I'll have the bailiff clear the coatroom.' "

Connoisseur: "I says to my friend Ramon, 'Man you really stink today, what connoisseur did you crawl out of?' "

Copulate: "I called 911, and an hour later, when they showed up, I said copulate."

Data: "At my basketball game the other night, I score a triple double and my coach said data boy, Darnell."

Decide: "My favorite girls are Wanda and Yolanda, but I like to keep a couple on decide.

Derange: "Derange is where the deer and the antelope play."

Dimension: "A lot of you ladies been calling in, wondering what Darnell look like. Well, he tall, dark, handsome, not dimension, hung like a horse."

Disappointment: "My parole officer told me if I miss disappointment, he's going to send me back to the big house."

Fascinate: "My sister Wolanda bought a sweater with ten buttons on it, but her tits are so big, she can only fascinate."

Foreclose: "If I don't pay my alimony this month, I'll have more money foreclose."

Formaldehyde: "The police came to my door looking for my cousin Melvin. I told them there ain't no place formaldehyde in the house, it be too small."

Fortify: "I asked this bitch down on Six Mile—How much? She said fortify dollars, honey."

Homo: "The bitch I'm living with called me at the bar the other night. She said, 'Darnell, honey, are you coming homo, what?' "

Honor: "At our rape trial, the judge asked my buddy Jarvis who be honor?"

Horde: "My mama always did have a bad reputation 'cause she horde around in her school."

Income: "My girlfriend and I just got into bed, when income my wife."

July: "After the trial, my mama asked me, 'Did you tell the truth or July?' "

Letter: "The ugly bitch downstairs came knocking on Darnell's door the other night, and I wouldn't letter in."

Manual: "I told my buddy Tyrone, 'Manual get yourself in trouble if you keep messing with that hoe.' "

Menstruate: "With the fashions today, you can't keep the women and menstruate."

Odyssey: "When I got back from the Windsor Ballet, I told my friends, you Odyssey the tits on that babe."

Oral: "My friend Sebastian said, 'Give me twenty-five cents oral blow your head off.' "

Oreo: "I told my friend, Alonzo, if he wanted my sister, he could pay me fifty bucks now oreo me one hundred bucks on Friday."

Orgasm: "I asked my cousin Dexter about the death penalty in his state. I asked if they electrocute 'em, hang, orgasm."

Penis: "I saw my parole officer the other day and he handed me a little paper cup and said, 'Here, penis.' "

Polyp: "On my way home from the Piston's game the other night, I was involved in a five-car polyp on I-75."

Rectum: "I had two Cadillacs, but my girlfriend rectum both."

Seldom: "I had two extra tickets to the basketball game the other night, so I seldom to my friends."

Semen: "I never did know who my papa was 'cause my mama semen left and right."

Sodomy: "When I go out at night, I like to have a bitch on one sodomy and another bitch on the other sodomy."

Stain: "My sister and brother-in-law stopped by the other day, so I asked them, 'You plannin' on stain?' "

Undermine: "There's a fine looking bitch living in the apartment right undermine.

Urinal: "After the police broke down my front door last night, they said, 'Darnell, urinal lot of trouble.' "

Widen: "When my girlfriend, Larina, told me she was pregnant, I said, 'Widen you tell me you didn't use no birth control?' "

FUCK IS THE MOST USEFUL WORD IN THE ENGLISH LANGUAGE

Aggression	Fuck you.
Disbelief	Unfuckinbelievable.
Dismay	Ah, fuck it.
Displeasure	What the fuck is going on here?
Fraud	I got fucked at the poker game.
Greeting	How the fuck are you?
Ignorance	What the fuck is this all about?
Incompetence	He fucks up everything.
Lost	Where in the fuck are we?
Love	I really fucking love you, baby.
Pleasure	What a great fuck that was.
Retaliation	Up your fucking ass, faggot.
Trouble	Well, I guess I'm totally fucked now.
Rebellion	Fuck you, mom. I'm going out, anyway.

THE ALL-TIME YOU SO UGLY LIST

YOU SO UGLY THAT:

—Your bitch makes you wear a bag over your head when you fuck her.

—Your own dick won't even let you touch it

—You went to a haunted house and came out with an application.

—You could model for death threats.

—When you were born they put tinted windows on your incubator.

—You have to sneak up on your mirror.

—When you sit in the sand, the cats try to bury you.

—The only doctor see you is a Vet.

—When you were born the doctor took one look at you and slapped your parents.

—You stuck your head out of the car window and got arrested for mooning.

—You have to trick or treat by phone.

—When your mother went into labor, your father went into shock.

—Every time your mother looks at you she says to herself, "Damn, I should've just given head."

—They call you Taco Bell; when people see you they run for the border.

—You make onions cry.

—The tide wouldn't bring you in.

—When I took you to see the zookeeper, he said, "Thanks for bringing him back."

—You mother had to get drunk before she breast-fed you.

—You went to a freak show and got a permanent job.

—You make blind kids cry.

—Farmers use your picture as a scarecrow.

—Every time you go out, you get chased by the dog-catcher.

—When you jerk off, your hand tries to fall asleep.

—When you threw a boomerang, it didn't come back.

—You can't get a date off the calendar.

—When your mother went into labor, the doctors went on strike.

—Your last name is Link and your first is Missing.

—People put your picture in their car window, and nobody'll come near it.

THE TOP SIXTEEN EUPHEMISMS FOR MASTURBATION

16. Lap-based web browsing.
15. Gettin' some air nookie.
14. Wrangling the invertebrate serpent.
13. Polishing the skin flute.
12. Jostling the elder.
11. Ruminating and poundering.
10. Shaking your fist at the exgirlfriend.
9. Releasing the hostages.
8. Tickling your elmo.
7. Fixing the hubble.
6. Putting the seminal luge team through their paces.
5. Milking the snake.
4. Beta-testing the hardware.
3. Downloading from your own website.
2. Evicting the testicular squatters.

AND THE NUMBER ONE EUPHEMISM FOR MASTURBATION . . .

1. MISTSFCRLM (Manually Increasing the Surface Temperature of the Ship's Primary Cannon by Repeated Linear Manipulation)